82nd Airborne in Normandy

82nd Airborne in Normandy

A History in Period Photographs

Dominique François

Schiffer Military History
Atglen, PA

Dedication

This book is dedicated to the 82nd Airborne Division soldiers of World War II.

Special Thanks to:

General Paul F.Smith (507th PIR), OB.Hill (508th PIR), Marcus Heim (505th PIR), Colonel Wayne Pierce (325th GIR), Colonel Luis Mendez (508th PIR), Colonel Frank Naughton (507th PIR), Lou Horn (507th PIR), Jack Schlegel (508th PIR), General Ed Thomas (505th PIR), Colonel Tom Shanley (508th PIR), Lt.Colonel Chet Graham (508th PIR), Lt.Colonel Gordon K.Smith (507th PIR), Colonel Dave Brummit (507th PIR), Marvin T. Williams (507th PIR), S.R. Hartline (325th GIR), Frank Staple (508th PIR), Jim Mc. Callum (505th PIR), E.F."Buck" Waddell, Bill Nation, Marty Morgan, Kristine Nymoen, Remy Bouron, James Terrell ect.

Book Design by Ian Robertson.

Library of Congress Control Number: 2004105870

Printed in China.
ISBN: 0-7643-2057-2

We are interested in hearing from authors with book ideas on related topics.

Published by Schiffer Publishing Ltd.
4880 Lower Valley Road
Atglen, PA 19310
Phone: (610) 593-1777
FAX: (610) 593-2002
E-mail: Info@schifferbooks.com.
Visit our web site at: www.schifferbooks.com
Please write for a free catalog.
This book may be purchased from the publisher.
Please include $3.95 postage.
Try your bookstore first.

In Europe, Schiffer books are distributed by:
Bushwood Books
6 Marksbury Avenue
Kew Gardens
Surrey TW9 4JF
England
Phone: 44 (0) 20 8392-8585
FAX: 44 (0) 20 8392-9876
E-mail: Bushwd@aol.com.
Free postage in the UK. Europe: air mail at cost.
Try your bookstore first.

Contents

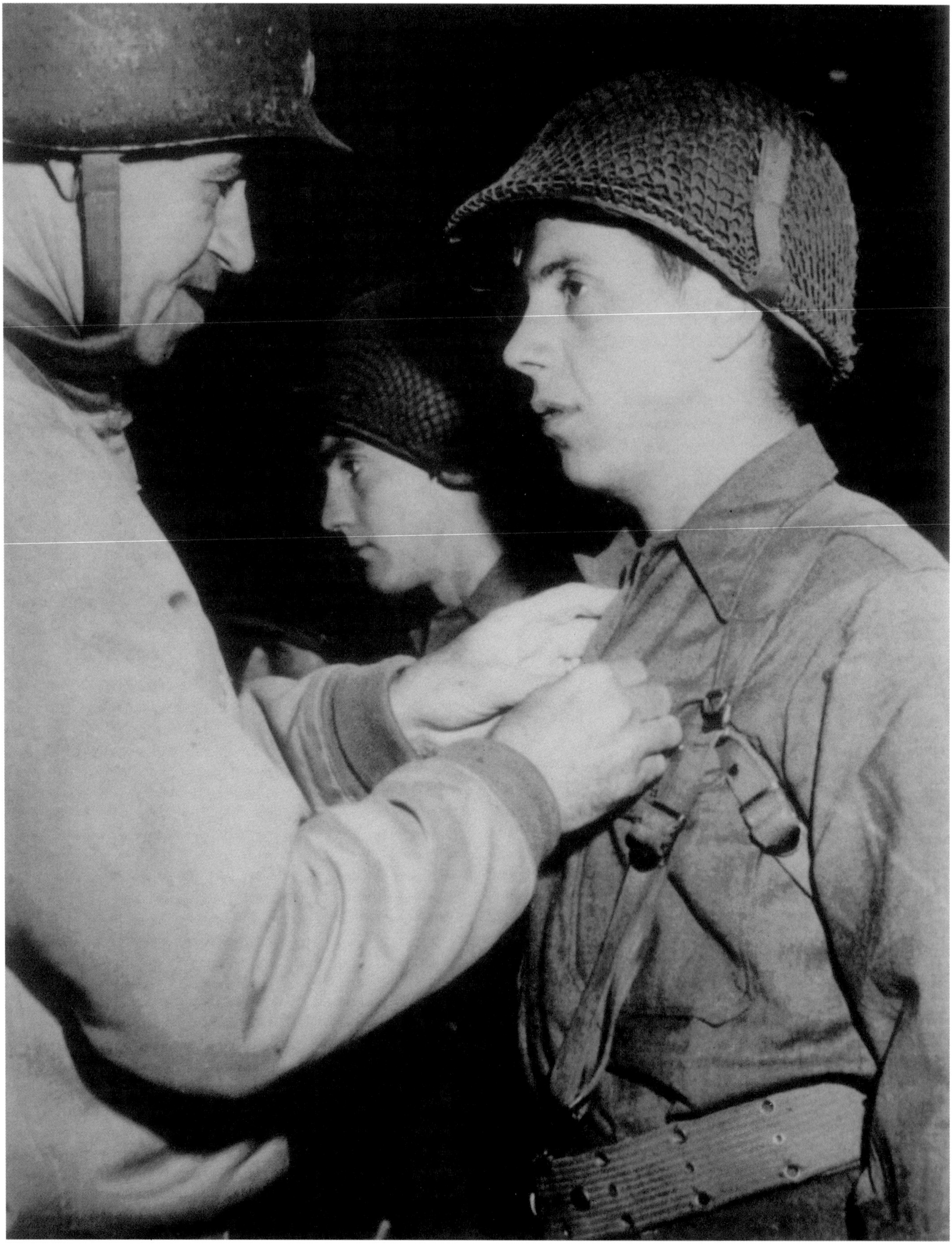

Preface

Thousands upon thousands have returned to books that tell the stories of the men and women who were in World War II. The author of this book is Dominique Francois, who lives in Normandy. I have met Dominique many times, both in France and United States. He is a great historian and a good friend of all Airborne Divisions. He has researched extensively all the airborne activities in Africa and Europe during World War II. This book, on the 82nd Airborne Division during that time, is as accurate as possible. I joined the 505th PIR in December 1943 as a replacement at Cookstown, North Ireland. I was assigned to a bazooka team, and I stayed with the 505 from 1943 until the end of the war in Europe. I jumped in Normandy and Holland and saw action in Belgium and Germany. The toll was heavy, and we lost many of our comrades; men who were family to us, who we depended on in combat, and who helped us overcome the Germans. It was our trust and faith in each other that helped us get through some very difficult times. Everyone feels proud of their outfit—especially ours—but never so pround as when we were chosen to be the Guard of Honor for the Headquarters Allied Expeditionary Forces in Europe. The American people here in the United States read about and saw many pictures of the hardships that the people in France, Holland, and Belgium had endured under four years of German occupation. Some had their homes destroyed, many lost family and loved ones, and yet they thank us for their freedom. Every time I go to France, Holland, or Belgium I meet someone who was living during WWII, and they all remember D-Day and the freedom that they got back, and thank us over and over with tears in their eyes. As you read this history of the 82nd Airborne Division that Dominique has put together and come to realize all the men who were left behind, those who lost parts of their body, and those who have flashbacks of horrible memories from the war, say a prayer for them that we may find a way to have peace in the World.

Dedicated to our falling heroes of WWII. Some lie asleep at Sicily, while others are at Normandy and in the Ardennes. Some gave their lives in Holland, and so their story ends. But the story that comes from the boys of the 82nd will tell of their hardship and suffering, and how they tried to stay alive. "Geronimo!" was their bye-word, onward with a trust. God grant that we will always remember our Comrades who sleep in the dust. God bless America and all peace loving countries in the World.

Marcus Heim
Co A, 1st Bn, 505th PIR/ 82nd ABN Div. (DSC)

Opposite: General Omar Bradley presents to Marcus Heim (505th PIR) the Distinguished Service Cross for his bravery in the combats during the Battle of La Fiére.

1

Reactivation and Training

The thought of an airborne division was called a fantastic dream in 1940. Only Russia would waste men that way. But the Japaneses came along with a sneak play and turned Pearl Harbor into an inferno. So the 82nd Infantry Division was reactivated on 25 March 1942 at Camp Claiborne, Louisiana, under the command of Major General Omar N. Bradley. The Division commenced training under doctrines appropriate for a standard infantry division. Major General Matthew B. Ridgway took command on 26 June 1942 and continued the work of his predecessor.

The Airborne idea was gaining more adherents every day. The 82nd, under the wise leadership and skillful handling of its commander, soon developed into the most promising among the new units being quickly whipped into shape. On the 15th day of August, what so many thought was just a nasty rumor became stark reality. On that day the 82nd was designated as an Airborne Division, and one half its strength was subtracted to form the 101st Airborne Division. Later the 82nd surrendered a full quota of key personnel to cadre the 98th Infantry Division.

The reorganized division consisted of the 325th and 326th Glider Infantry Regiments and the 319th and 320th Glider Field Artillery Battalions. These and normal service units were composed of personnel who had never dreamed of being airborne. The 504th Parachute Infantry Regiment and the 376th Field Artillery Battalion were added to the new division, and the Engineer battalion was reconstitued with two companies of glider designation and one of parachutists. Special troop units were appropritely changed in strength and organization for airborne operation.

Ground training of the Division continued at Camp Claiborne until 1 October 1942, when the bulk of the unit was moved to Fort Bragg, North Carolina, in the largest airborne troop movement ever attempted in a single operation. At the new station, thousands of new recruits were given basic training and integrated into the glider elements. Advanced ground training alternated with flight exercices by both troop transport and parachute, and by troop transport and gliders were pushed vigorously.

The sturdy and reliable C-47 was doing a wonderful job for the paratroopers, but production lines had not revved into high gear yet to turn out bug-proof gliders fast enough. This made a further change in the organization of the division necessary if it was going to be ready for early overseas shipment. On 12 February 1943 the 326th Glider Infantry Regiment was withdrawn from the Division and replaced by the 505th Parachute Infantry Regiment. To balance this change and permit organization of regimental combat teams, Company "B" of the 307th Airborne Engineer Battalion was converted from glider to parachute status. The 456th Parachute Field Artillery Battalion was added for the same reason.

The 82nd Airborne Division arrived in the European Theater of Operations on 9 December 1943, bronzed by the summer sun of North Africa and Sicily and bled and battle-tested in campaigns in Sicily and the Italian mainland. One Regimental Combat Team (the 504th) had been left behind when the Division sailed from Naples, Italy, on 19 November 1943.

The 504th Regimental Combat team (consisting of the 504th Parachute Infantry, the 376th Parachute Field Artillery Battalion, and Company C, 307th Airborne Engineer Battalion) was detached from the Division and was fighting in the mountains north of the Volturno River when the 82nd sailed from Naples.

Later it was to spend more than 60 days of gruelling warfare on the famous Anzio Beachhead before rejoining the Division in England in May.

The Division disembarked at Belfast, Northern Ireland, and occupied an area northwest of that city. Division Headquaters was established at Castle Dawson, which was approximately thirty miles from Belfast. The Division was attached to XV Corps.

A shortage of adequate training facilities, the short days and long nights, and no facilities at all for airborne maneuvers handicapped training. The need for such facilities and training became increasingly important with the attachment to the Division on 14 January 1944 of the 2nd Airborne Brigade, which included the Brigade Headquarters and Headquaters Company and the 507th and the 508th Parachute Infantry Regiments. Preparations were then made for the 82nd to move to Nottingham, Leicester, Market Harbord area in the English Midlands. Brigadier General Maxwell B. Taylor, Division Artillery Commander, rejoined the Division after duty in the North African Theater of Operations.

The move to the Midlands was made in mid-February 1944, and an intensive program of airborne and other types of training was begun. A parachute school was opened to train reinforcements, and a series of parachute problems was mapped out, beginning with battalion drops and culminating with a drop of three regiments. Glider personnel trained with the British Horsa gliders, as well as with the CG-4A (Waco) gliders, took training rides of more than two hours duration.

Division Headquaters was established in a hutted camp in Braunstone Park, Leicester. The telephone code names of "Leader" and "Keystone"—employed by the Division in North Africa, Sicily, and Italy—were dropped, and the Division became know as " Champion." The 456th Parachute Field Artillery Battalion, which had seen much of its personnel detached and left in Italy, was reorganized. The 2nd Battalion, 401st Glider Infantry, 101st Airborne Division, was attached to the 325th Glider Infantry. This move gave the 325th a total of three battalions. Brigadier General Taylor left the Division to become Commanding General of the 101st Airborne Division. The Division was attached to the VIII Corps.

Meanwhile, preparations were being made for the Division's participation in the invasion of the Normandy, France, Peninsula by Allied forces in "Operation Neptune." Brigadier General James M. Gavin, the assistant Division Commander, had proceded the Division on its move from Italy and had been a member of the airborne planning staff established by the Allies in London. The Division staff began preliminary planning work in January and started intensive planning in February, when the Division Situation Room was opened at Camp Braunstone. The Division Commander, Major General Matthew B. Ridgway, was the senior American Airborne representative on an inter-Allied airborne planning committee.

"Y-Day," the day by which all plans were to be completed, had been set by Supreme Headquarters, Allied Expeditionary Force, as 1 June. Regimental staffs were "briefed" on Y-60 and battalion staffs on Y-30 in accordance with instructions received from the First United States Army and VII Corps, to which the Division would be attached upon landing.

Three paratroopers with M.1941 jump suits in 1941 at Fort Benning; on the left is Fred Carden.

Fred Carden in early 1941 with his T-4 parachute and wearing the Herringbone twill mechanic's coveralls with nametape.

A paratrooper is waiting for orders to go to Salerno, Sicily, September 1943.

Colonel Roy Linquist, Commanding Officer of the 508th PIR, with Major Shanley at Fort Benning in 1942.

507th troopers during Tenessee manoeuvers.

A trooper poses in the door at Fort Benning.

Two generations of paratroopers, father and son.

General Marschall inspects Fort Benning School.

250 foot tower at Fort Benning.

A 34 foot tower.

The Three 250-foot towers at Fort Benning.

Above: This wind trainer was used to give trainees experience in subduing a wind-blown canopy (Fort Benning). Below: Many civilian and military visitors would come to visit the new Airborne school.

General Marshall with the instructor of the jump school of Fort Benning.

Individual equipment for a parachute rifleman.

A paratrooper with radio equipment.

Sgt. Carl Letson at the end of the war.

Colonel Roy Lindquist, commanding the 508th PIR, observes the training of his men at Fort Benning in 1943.

Two soldiers of a mortar detachment of the 508th PIR.

Patch of the 82nd Airborne Division.

Patch of the Airborne Command.

507th PIR shoulder and pocket patch, and Airborne wing background.

Cap Badges para/glider (left: officer, right: enlisted man).

Above: 508th PIR shoulder and pocket patch, and airborne wing background.

Parachute cap badges, left to right: Parachute Infantry, Parachute artillery and engineers, and Parachute Infantry.

Paratroopers wearing the Riddell plastic helmet, August 1943.

An Argentine officer inspects Fort Benning.

This paratrooper has made his first jump at Fort Benning; he wears the Riddell helmet.

Two 507th PIR paratroopers load a 60mm mortar during training.

Propaganda poster representing the U.S. Airborne Troops.

Propaganda poster for a fund raising.

Propaganda poster.

One of the jump towers at Fort Benning.

Left to right: Brig.Gen. Donovan, Commanding General of the 1st Airborne Brigade; Maj.Gen.Chapman, Commanding Gen. Airborne Command; Colonel Millett, Commanding Officer of the 507th PIR; and Pfc Clifford C.Worme, Hq&Hq Co, 507th PIR.

T5 parachute damaged during a training jump. The paratrooper did not survive the fall.

View of a paratrooper's equipment. He carries a PM Thompson that he has placed behind his equipment, ready to be used.

Cpl. Koward Huebner of the 507th PIR.

On the first days of combat, the A5 bundles are the only means for supplying ammunition.

Fort Benning, 1943. T-5 parachutes are distributed to the paratroopers for training jumps.

Before being placed in the bundles, the machine guns are greased. This photograph was taken in the tented camp at Nottingham, England.

Training jump in the United States.

Training jump at Fort Benning. The first parachutes used had white canopies.

A stick of the 507th PIR is jumping during maneuvers in Tennessee.

Beautiful photograph of an exit of a C-47 during a training jump in the USA.

This picture shows the position of a paratrooper at the airplane door. This trooper placed his U.S. M1A1 rifle under his harness, and did not use the weapon's protecting cover.

Above and following: Diverse sequences of the dropping of a 507th PIR Medic stick during a training jump in the USA.

Paratroopers of the 508th PIR on the Lions of City Hall in Nottingham, England, after the Battle of Normandy.

2

Plans and Missions

By 26 May 1944 all plans and preparations were completed for the Division to carry out the missions assigned to it by the First United States Army. Fields and administrative orders had been published and distributed. In a series of map maneuvers on a special 1/5,000 map, regimental and battalion commanders had outlined their plans so that all commanders could be briefed thoroughly on their prospective Division operations. Divisional seaborne echelons already had departed for the marshalling yards and were assembled in camps scattered along the Welsh and Southern English coasts. The Division missions were to be as follows:

"Land by parachute and glider before and after dawn of D-Day west of St. Sauveur le Vicomte, seize, clear and secure the general area St.Jacques de Nehou-Besneville (both inclusive)—St. Sauveur le Vicomte (exclusive— Blandamour (inclusive) and reorganize; seize and destroy the crossings of the 'Prairies marecageuse' north of La Sangsuriere at St. Sauveur de Pierremont; destroy the crossings of the Ollononde River in the vicinity of St. Lo d'Ourville and block crossroads vicinity Le Chemin; prevent enemy forces moving north between St. Lo d'Ourville and junction of Douve River with 'Prairies marecageuse'; and protect the south flank of VII Corps north of the same line."

The mission, however, was changed by the First Army Commander on 26 May due to confirmed intelligence reports that the enemy had strengthened his forces on the Cotentin Peninsula with the addition of the 91st Infantry Division in the general area of St. Sauveur le Vicomte. The revised mission of the 82nd Airborne Division was to be as follows:

"Land by parachute and glider before and after dawn of D-Day astride the Merderet River, seize, clear and secure the general area: Neuville au Plain, Baudienville, within its zone; capture Ste Mere Eglise; seize and secure the crossings of the Merderet River at La Fiere and Chef du Pont and a bridgehead covering them, with MLR along the general line; seize and destroy the crossings of the Douve River at Beuzevillie la Bastille and Etienville; protect the northwest flank of VII Corps within the Division zone; and be prepared to advance west on Corps order to the line of the Douve north of its junction with the 'Prairies Marecageuses.'"

New Orders and other administrative details made necessary by the new mission were worked out quickly and disseminated within few days. The change did not affect the basic plan for movement in the three echelons, which had been worked out as follows:

The 507th PIR parades on a Northern Ireland beach. It is soon to be sent to Nottingham, England.

Force "A": commanded by brigadier General James M. Gavin, assistant Division Commander, to be committed by parachute before dawn of D-Day and to include:

Units	Planes
Det. HQ & HQ Co, 82nd Airborne Division	4
Pathfinders	9
Det. HQ 82nd Div. Artillery	2
Det. 82nd Abn. Signal Corp	3
Det. 456 Parachute FA Battalion (attached 505 PIR)	
Air Support Party (attached HQ 82nd Abn Div.)	
505th Parachute Infantry Regiment	117
507th Parachute Infantry Regiment	117
508th Parachute Infantry Regiment	117
Co B, 307th Abn Engineer Battalion	9
Naval Shore Fire Control Party (attached 505th PIR)	
Total	378

Force "B": commanded by Major General Matthew B. Ridgway, Division Commander, to be committed by glider before and after dawn of D-Day and to include:

Units	Gliders
HQ & HQ Co 82nd Airborne Division	22
HQ & HQ Battery, 82nd Airborne Division Artillery	11
82nd Airborne Signal Corp	13
325th Glider Infantry Regiment	172
319th Glider Field Artillery Battalion	40
320th Glider Field Artillery Battalion	54
Batterys A, B, C, 80th Airborne AA Battalion	57
Co A, 307th Airborne Engineer Battalion	10
307th Airborne Medical Co	20
82nd Airborne Recon Platoon	13
Air Support Party	4
Command vehicles- Parachutes Regiments	12
Total	428

Force "C": commanded by Brigadier General George P. Howell, commanding General of 2nd Airborne Infantry Brigade, to be committed by sea, to land between D plus 2 and D plus 7 and include:

456 Field Artillery Battalion
80th Airborne Antiaircraft Battalion
307th Airborne Engineer Battalion
782th Airborne Ord. Maintenance Co.
407th Airborne Quarter Master Co.
82nd Airborne Military Police Platoon
Corps Medical Dets.
87th Armored FA Battalion (attached)
899th TD Battalion (attached)
Tr B, 4th Cav. Sqadron (attached)
Co C, 746th Tank Battalion (attached)
3809 QM Trk Co (attached)
3810 QM Trk Co (attached)
1st Platoon, 603rd QM Co (attached)

Under the plan Force "A" in its entirety was to approach the Cotentin Peninsula from the west and drop between 0100 and 0315 hours on the night of D-1/D-Day on three drop zones. The 505th Parachute Infantry Regiment and its attachments were to land east of the Merderet River, about 1,000 yards northwest of Sainte Mere Eglise. The 507th Parachute Infantry Regiment was to land west of the Merderet River, about 1,000 yards north of Amfreville. The 508th Parachute Infantry Regiment and Force "A" Headquarters were to land west of the Merderet River, about 1,000 yards north of Picauville.

Fifty-two gliders of Force "B" were to approach the Cotentin Peninsula from the west prior to H-Hour and land on the 505th drop zone. The remainder of Force "B" was to approach the Peninsula

The elected officials of Nottingham, England, greet the 507th PIR soldiers.

from the east and was to land late on D-Day and early on D plus one on Landing Zones astride the Sainte Mere Eglise-Blosville road. In a last-minute change of plans General Ridgway parachuted with Force "A."

Aerial resupply missions were scheduled automatically for the morning of D plus one and on call thereafter if needed. The automatic mission was the only parachute mission ultimately flown, but a small amount of equipment and supplies were received later by glider.

All airborne elements of the Division had closed and were sealed in special camps at the take-off fields by 24 hours before the scheduled take-off time.

Parachute elements were located at seven airfields in the Grantham - Cottesmore - Langar area of the British Middlands, and glider elements were at seven airfields in the Aldermaston - Ramsbury - Merryfields area.

All men were briefed theroughly on their missions, a recheck was made of all equipment and personnel, and planes and gliders were loaded with equipment. The Allied D-Day was postponed 24 hours because of weather conditions, and the first planes of Force "A" took off at 2315 on June 5, 1944.

The main flight was preceded by the three regimental pathfinder teams, which dropped one-half hour prior to the first group. The pathfinders sustained many casualties and had difficulty in using lights, but they accomplished their mission and set up beacons to guide the incoming planes to the three designated drop zones.

The flight over the English Channel was in good formation and without incident, but between the west coast and the drop zones a heavy fog bank tended to break up the formation of the planes. Flak and some enemy fighter activity caused some of the troop carrier planes to take evasive actions, and by the time the drop zones were reached many planes were scattered, flying at excessive speeds and at altitudes higher than ideal for jumping.

The 505th Parachute Infantry Regiment landed in the general vicinity of its drop zone. The 507th Parachute Infantry Regiment was scattered; one element dropped in the vicinity of Valognes (Negreville), another south of Carentan (Graignes), and the remainder astride the Merderet River, east of the drop zone. The 508th Parachute Infantry Regiment was likewise scattered widely, the bulk of its parachutists dropping east of the drop zone, and some personnel landing as far away as nine kilometers south of Cherbourg.

The 52 gliders containing batteries of the 80th Airborne Antiaircraft Battalion and detachments and forward parties of artillery, signal, and Division Headquarters groups followed the main body of paratroopers and began landing at 0404 hours. The gliders also encountered fog and flak. They too were scattered, and many of them were damaged upon crashing into the small fields and high hedgerows.

Ennemy reaction to the landing of the 82nd Airborne Division in the Normandy area was prompt and severe, but from the time the first member landed until 33 days later, when the Division was finally relieved, every mission was accomplished, and no ground gained was ever relinquished.

508th
Parachute Infantry
Regiment

ORGANIZATION DAY

Colonel Roy E. Lindquist
Commanding

NOVEMBER FOURTH
1943

Booklet delivered for the first anniversary of the 508th PIR, November 4, 1943.

Rare color photograph taken at Fort Benning during a training jump.

Paratroopers of the 507th PIR in contact by radio during maneuvers in Tennessee.

Paratroopers of the 82nd Airborne Division on a North African airfield, shortly before the departure for Sicily.

In England, a few hours before departing to Normandy, thousands of C-47 and gliders awaiting take-off.

A few minutes before departure, the paratroopers of the 82nd Airborne wait for boarding.

Sgt. Thomas J. Blakey of the 1st Bn. 505th PIR at Camp Tacoa, Georgia, in 1943, behind the wheel of an experimental Jeep that was being tested for Airborne service. (Courtesy Marty Morgan)

Above and following: Booklet distributed to all paratroopers of the 82nd Airborne Division.

AIRBORNE

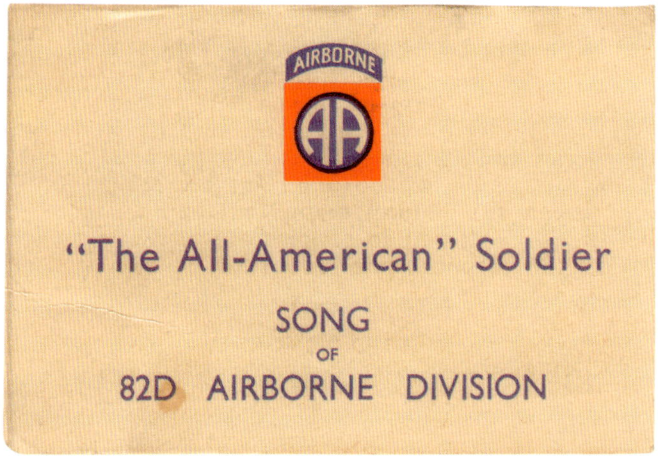

Song of the 82nd Airborne Division.

A group of 507th PIR paratroopers of the Intelligence section, showing the different weapons used by this team: USM1 Rifle; USM1 A1 rifle; and Thompson Submachine gun.

Three paratroopers of the 507th PIR Intelligence section.

The 507th PIR Intelligence section. They carry Thompsons and have many rigger made equipments.

Sgt. Carlson Smith, demolitions platoon, with Geronimo.

Sgt Carlson Smith (left), 507th PIR, and Dub Murray (right), KIA at Graignes.

Pfc. Jack Summer, 507th PIR.

Lt. Donald O. Graul, 507th PIR, was later captured in Normandy.

Seaborne land at Utah Beach on 6 June.

Paratroopers of the 508th PIR in France, in the Sissonne area.

A group of paratroopers of the 508th PIR after the combats of Normandy and Holland, before departing for the Ardennes.

A few weeks before D-Day, these paratroopers received their jump uniforms modified by the riggers. Note the piles of reinforced outfits in the background.

T/4 Joseph Gorenc, HHC, 506th, hoists his bulky load aboard.

Utah Beach.

A stick of the 508th PIR during a training jump.

Conrad Wolfe of the 508th PIR Company D about to board for the Market Garden Operation.

Warren Albright of the 508th PIR Company D.

Tom McBlane of the 508th PIR Company D.

This 508th PIR paratrooper is waiting on an airfield in England to get equipped and leave for Normandy.

Post cards of Camp Mackall in North Carolina.

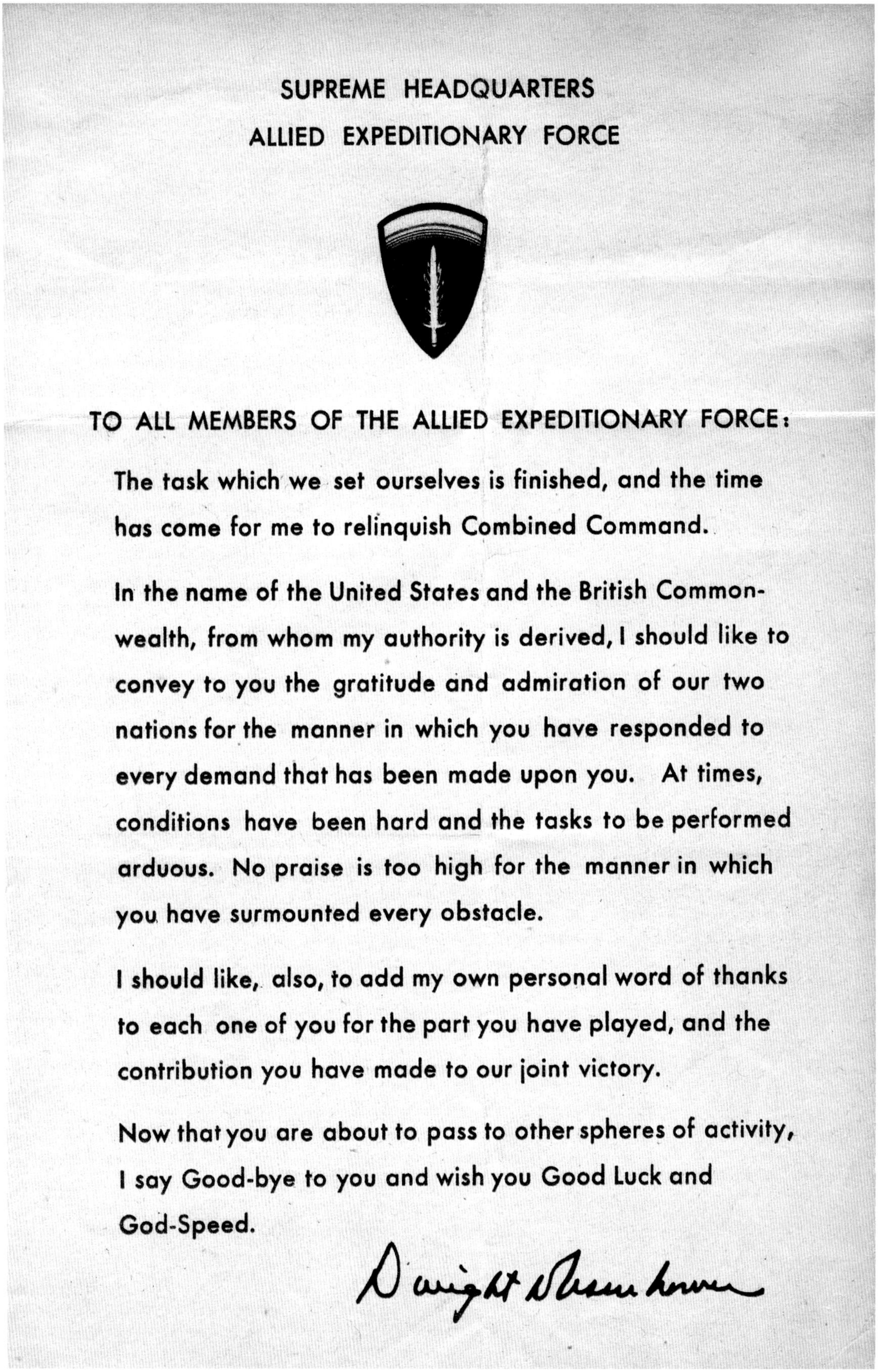

SUPREME HEADQUARTERS
ALLIED EXPEDITIONARY FORCE

TO ALL MEMBERS OF THE ALLIED EXPEDITIONARY FORCE:

The task which we set ourselves is finished, and the time has come for me to relinquish Combined Command.

In the name of the United States and the British Commonwealth, from whom my authority is derived, I should like to convey to you the gratitude and admiration of our two nations for the manner in which you have responded to every demand that has been made upon you. At times, conditions have been hard and the tasks to be performed arduous. No praise is too high for the manner in which you have surmounted every obstacle.

I should like, also, to add my own personal word of thanks to each one of you for the part you have played, and the contribution you have made to our joint victory.

Now that you are about to pass to other spheres of activity, I say Good-bye to you and wish you Good Luck and God-Speed.

Dwight Eisenhower

Pamphlet distributed to all soldiers participating in D-Day, signed by General Eisenhower.

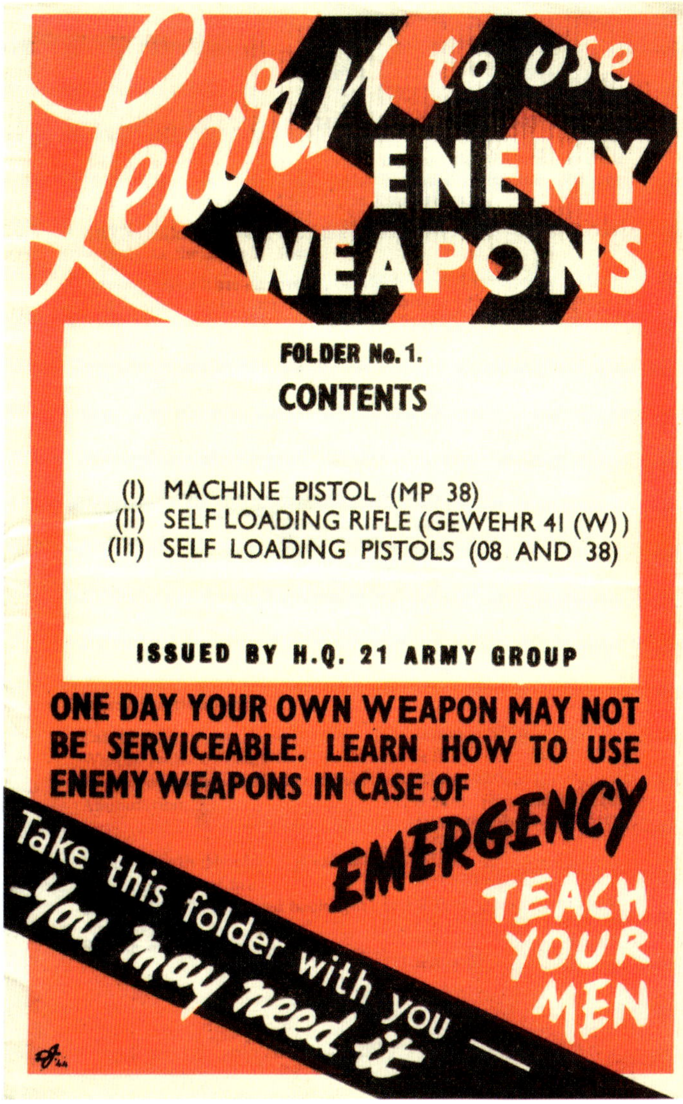

Booklet distributed a few days before D-Day to the paratroopers to teach them how to use the German weapons.

Interesting photograph showing a paratrooper of the 82nd Airborne Division carrying a 30 caliber machine gun in a Griswold Bag, as well as a U.S. M1 A1 rifle.

Loading of the guns belonging to the airborne artillery in Camp Mackall.

Airplane fuselage used for plane exit training.

Training for close-combat at Camp Blanding, Florida.

3

Normandy Day-by-Day

"...33 Days of action without relief, without replacements. Every mission accomplished. No ground gained ever relinquisted."

Major General Matthew B. Ridway

D-DAY, 6 June 1944

The first element of the main body of the Division jumped at 0151 hours, having been preceded 30 minutes by the Pathfinder teams. By 0312 hours all paratroopers had landed, and at 0404 hours the first of 52 gliders in the initial glider serial crash-landed. Both parachutists and gliders were scattered.

Small groups and some units attacked to secure the Division zone. Groups of men and individuals who had been scattered in the landings rejoined their units throughout the day, and by nightfall approximately 30 percent of the Division's forces were under control.

At 2100 hours 100 gliders landed with artillery, engineers, and special troops. Seaborne elements set sail at 0645 from Bristol, except for a task force consisting of Company C, 746th Tank Battalion, the 1st Platoon, Troop B, 4th Cavalry Squadron, and elements of Co F, 3rd Battalion (originally 2nd Battalion, 401st Glider Infantry) and the 325th Glider Infantry. This task force landed on Utah Red Beach at 1400 hours and procceded inland with the mission of contacting the Division near Sainte Mere Eglise.

At the close of the day the Division was in the midst of severe fighting. It had captured Sainte Mere Eglise and held a general line along the Merderet River from La Fiere south, to include the eastern end of the causeway over the merderet River.

Headquarters & Headquarters Company, 82nd Airborne Division

Parachute elements (part of Force "A") dropped at 0214 hours near the west bank of the Merderet River, and glider elements (loading echelon of Force "B") landed at 0204 hours. The Force "A" Command Post was set up initially west of the Merderet River, but at 0730 the group waded across the River to the east bank and assembled at La Fiere. A new Force "A" Command Post was established at a railroad crossing.

The Division Commander, who jumped with the 505th PIR, established his Command Post in a hedgerow west of Sainte Mere Eglise. Elements of Headquarters and of the Defense Platoon moved south to secure the bridge west of Chef du Pont, where it encountered severe enemy fire. This group returned to the Command Post at 1700, but part of the Defense Platoon moved to a new Force "A" Command Post at a railroad pass.

505th Parachute Infantry Regiment

Lt. Colonel Benjamin Vandervoort, 2nd Bn, 505th PIR

"...The flight until we hit the French coast was quite uneventful for my Battalion. We reached France intact and in formation. As we came in across the coast we saw a little ack-ack from the ground, and I thought that there were some planes from the 101st Division shot down. As we approached our DZ the pilot informed me that he could see our T. The pathfinder group had been dropped essentially where they should have been, a little further inland, and they only displayed two Ts. One was lighted when we dropped. The pilot I had was extremely reluctant to come down to the correct jumping altitude. We came in at 1400 feet, and our speed was excessive. I talked to the crew chief and asked him to slow down. We went through a bit of scud as we came in, and it caused the formation to break slightly. At the time I thought the Germans had smoked the area. I lost two platoons from Company 'F.' The green light was turned on about 45 seconds before we reached the Douve River. I told them to turn it off. We dropped

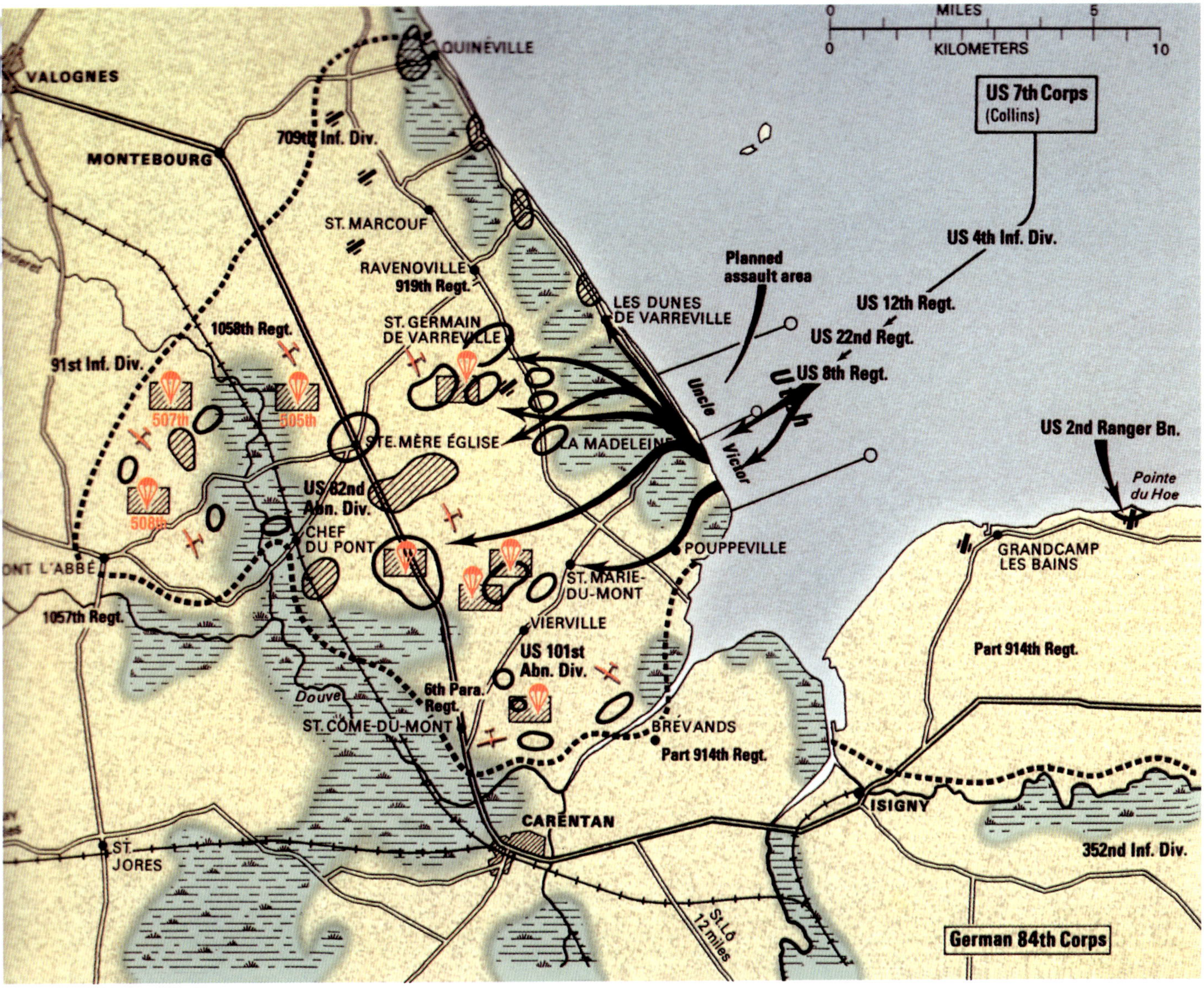

Map locating the different units engaged in Neptune.

pretty well on our DZ. I, myself, was a quarter of a mile from the DZ, and I had a little hard luck on the landing and banged up my foot. I watched the battalion come in, and they were well spread out, the ships being too high and too fast. Within fifteen minutes after I got on the ground I started putting up some green flares that worked out well. We encountered no resistance from the enemy at night, only some fire from ack-ack around the DZ. Some members of the Battalion were dropped in Sainte Mere Eglise and were engaged in a firefight at once. There was movement of vehicles on the road, one of the first things I heard being vehicles moving on a road to the south. I went north to the nearest hedgerow. I think it was about 0410 in the morning when I felt I completed the assembly sufficiently so that I could move out on our mission and take the town of Neuville Au Plain. In the meantime, the regiment had told me to stand by. The news from Sainte Mere Eglise to the Regimental commander was so vague that he had me stand by. General Ridgway happened to be in my CP during that period, and he also directed me not to move without consulting him. It was not until daylight that I received orders to move. We actually started moving at 0600. Later my mission was changed to Sainte Mere Eglise, and from there on it was essentially a ground operation..."

The first element (2nd Battalion, Lt.Colonel Benjamin H. Vandervoort) dropped at 0151 hours, and the entire regiment landed by 0202 hours. Most of the troops landed on or near the drop zone, but a few were widely dispersed over the countryside. Assembly was rapid, and the battalions moved off toward their objectives.

The 3rd Battalion (Lt. Colonel Edward C. Krause) entered Sainte Mere Eglise at 0400 hours, and the town was securely held and outposted within an hour. The American Flag was raised over Sainte Mere Eglise, the first French town to be liberated by the Allies. After assembling the 2nd Battalion started to move out to take Neuville Au Plain, but orders were received from the regiment to stand by. At 0600 hours the 2nd Battalion moved into position north of Sainte Mere Eglise and assisted the 3rd Battalion in holding the town. The 1st Battalion (Lt. Colonel Frederick C. Kellam) moved toward its objective (the bridge over the Merderet River at La Fiere) at 0630 hours, and by 0830 held the eastern end of this bridge against heavy enemy fire from the western approaches.

James Mc Callum, F Co, 505th PIR

"...I landed in Sainte Mere Eglise. The plane pilots were supposed to fly at 500 feet to drop the troops close to each other, but the pilots were afraid of being shot down by ack ack or anti-aircraft guns, so they flew at 2,000 feet, which led to the troops being scattered miles away from each other instead of landing in a group. The first thing I did was roll my parachute up in a ball so Germans could not see it. I remember being on one side of a fence and hearing German hob-nail boots running down the street on the other side of the fence 3 meters away—I was unseen by german soldiers. I headed to the house and exited the fence gate by the house and looked for friends. I crawled through the alley to a field, where I met two friends, Don Marino and another person whom I do not remember. An hour later I was walking around with Don Marino and the other guy when Don saw a helmet with netting or strips of cloth camo on it. In North Africa the German soldiers had nets on their helmets, so during previous months that net and camo was a German thing. Don Marino didn't say anything—he may have used the clicker but got no response. Don drew his 45 pistol and fired once. Then he heard in English "G** damn it, I got shot in the arm!" Then we realized it was a fellow American..."

507th Parachute Infantry Regiment

The first element (1st Battalion, Lt. Colonel Edwin J. Ostberg) jumped at 0232 hours, and by 0312 hours the entire regiment was on the ground generally cast of the Merderet River and was fairly dispersed. Small groups assembled to form small task forces until such time as the regiment could assemble completely. One such forces until such time as the regiment could assemble completely. One such force on the west bank of the Merderet River attacked Amfreville, but was forced back by overhelming superiority in enemy strength to Hameau Flaux. A patrol (Lt. Levy) was sent to the western end of La Fiere Bridge, and contact was made with elements of the 505th PIR on the eastern end at 1430 hours. The enemy recaptured Hameau Flaux and drove this patrol from the western end of LA Fiere Bridge. Another force of the regiment (Capt. Floyd B. Schwartzwalder) joined with Force "A" Headquarters, and at 1130 attacked to secure the chef Du Pont Bridge, meeting extremely severe resistance. At the eastern end of the bridge, the remainder of this second force moved to an assembly area at 1715 hours in the vicinity of the railroad overpass. Still another group, led by the Regimental commander, Colonel George Millett, landed on or near the scheduled drop zone, but had no contact with other elements of the Division during the day.

George Leidenheimer, 507th

"...At 2:00 AM on D-day, June 6, 1944, I parachuted into Normandy with the 507th PIR. I was captured that morning but escaped alone that night.

At dawn on June 7 I walked into a building next to Valognes Catholic church. The large room was filled with sleeping children and two nuns. The Priest hid me in a small building in the back of the churchyard. That night, armed with a hatchet and a map given to me by the church people, I set out to find my regiment. After daybreak, from a distance of a couple of miles I witnessed Valognes being bombed by American planes. Many times I have thought of those kids at the church. Later that day a French fighter led me to three paratroopers belonging to the 504th PIR. The first thing they asked me was if could blow up a German radio tower. They said London wanted the tower taken out, but nobody knew how. That night we killed the German radiomen and blew the tower.

The following day we had a party in the woods with four pretty Valognes girls. However, that night the leader of the fighters, who worked for the Germans as a Red Cross worker, told us to move our location, because the Germans had found out where we were. On June 10 we found the German squad (10 men) and killed them. That day we left the fighters and headed to our Regiments. We lost one man walking through two German divisions..."

508th Parachute Infantry Regiment

OB. Hill, HQ Co, 1st Bn, 508th PIR

"....Prior to the jump into Normandy, my batallion was placed temporarily at Folkingham airstrip, in the Midlands of England. As I remember, we were there about 5 days preparing for the invasion. Prior to that time we did not know when or where we would be involved in any combat action.

At Folkingham we studied sand tables that had been prepared by our Intelligence crew, known as S-2 people. They had constructed the sand table to show where we were supposed to land. Buildings, fencerows, hedgerows, rivers, ect. were on the table to give us a good view of the area where we were supposed to land. We spent our time studying that scene, packing equipment bundles, cleaning our rifles, playing cards and shooting dice in the hangar building, attending movies, attending church services, and writing letters. The area was secure, and no one was permitted to leave for any purpose. We were fully ready to take off from the airstrip on June 4, but the weather forced a delay of one day. With blackened faces we loaded into the planes the evening of June 5.

Every man in every plane was fully loaded with everything that he thought he might need. We were taking rations and ammunition for 3 days. There were ample ammunitions there, and many of us took several bandoliers over the allotted amount. This proved to be a worthwhile move, because most of us landed far from the scheduled drop zone, and we were behind the German lines for days before getting back to our unit. We also carried land mines, gammon grenades, maps, radios, smoke grenades, phohorous grenades, and more. Every man was fully loaded with every possible kind of equipment that might be needed.

At that time I was the 1st Bn. Message Center Chief with the rank of Buck Sergeant. Normally I would have jumped behind my Company Commander, Captain Gerard A. Ruddy. He and my platoon leader, 1st Lt.Charles J. Mc Elligott, were very good friends, and Mac wanted to jump behind Ruddy. As a result I traded spots in the plane with him, and I was then the last man to leave our plane. This proved to be a lucky break for me, because Captain Ruddy was killed very soon after landing, McElligott was shot through the stomach and captured, and most of the rest of those in the front of the plane were either killed or captured. McElligott is still around, and I thank him frequently for asking me to trade spots with him.

We left Folkingham at about 9:30 PM, as I remember. That is a pure guess, because to be honest, I was not wondering about the time as we loaded the plane and took off. We flew around for quite a long time getting all of the planes in formation for the flight across the channel. We could see planes in all directions around us during the formation period, and finally we were on our way to Normandy.

Our formation crossed the Guernsey Islands, and we started to see flak around us. As we hit the Normandy coast there was much more flak coming up from the antiaircraft batteries below us. The formation then hit some heavy clouds in addition to the flak. The combination of flak, clouds, and the inexperienced pilots was the reason for our biggest problem. The planes started veering right and left in order to be certain that they were not going to run into the planes on either side. We were standing up, all hooked up by this time, and when the green light went on, we jumped without knowing that we were not over the scheduled drop zones.

On the way down we were shot at with machine guns and rifles, and it looked very bad. We were not very high for the jump, but it seemed like forever before we reached the ground. On the way down I could see that there was lots of water below, and I assumed that it was the Merderet River; that was the river closest to where we were supposed to be. It later proved to be the Douve River, and I was to land about 5 miles from my scheduled drop zone. Also on the way down, some of the machine gun fire hit a gas mask case that I had strapped to my side. I had left the gas mask in England and filled the rubber mask case with cigarettes. The bullets ripped the case open, spun me around like a top, and ruined my cigarettes. I then landed in waist deep floodwaters, and they were still shooting at me.

When I first realized that I was going to land in the water I was sure that I would drown, because I had far too much equipment on me at that time. Because of all the extra weight that I carried I had to be helped into the plane. Many of us were loaded similarly. After hitting the water, I stood up and was just over waist deep. With the shooting still going on and bullets coming at me, I submerged again with just enough of me sticking out to allow me to breathe. The firing at me soon stopped, and I was able to assemble all of my gear and start getting out of the water...."

The 3rd Battalion (Lt. Colonel Louis Mendez) jumped at 0208 hours, and the entire regiment was on the ground by 0220 hours. Four separate groups were assembled. One group was in the vicinity of La Fiere, fought along the railway, and attacked the La Fiere Bridge. This group was later relieved by the 1st Battalion, 505th, and moved to an assembly area in the vicinity of the railroad overpass to organize a defensive position. The other groups joined forces west of the Merderet River, in the vicinity of Picauville, after taking part in heavy fighting around Gueutteville and north of Picauville. An officer of this group (Lt. Malcolm Brannen) shot and killed the commanding general of the German 91st Division. The combined group then seized the high ground west of the Merderet River, south of Gueutteville, during the night of June 6-7. A fourth group dropped in the vicinity of Sainte Mere Eglise and fought with the 507th to take the chef du Pont Bridge, and later organized a defensive position covering this bridge (Capt. Roy Creek).

Lieutenant Malcolm Brannen, Hq Co, 3rd Bn, 508th PIR

".... A corporal from the 2nd Bn 508th acted as my scout, and a private from the same company followed me; then two 307th Engineers brought up our rear; one was a sergeant—Clark I think. We came to a road running north and south, but did not dare to stay on it, so we crossed. We found some wire lines running along the road; the 307th engineers said they were communication lines, so I cut them in several places and took several yards of the wire and hid it so that the German linemen would have to patch the lines with wire that they carried, if they had any. Anyway, we figured that we had disrupted their communications for a while.

After following hedges north and east for a time we started due north again. During our journey we had seen C-47s after they had released gliders to go their way, and we also saw gliders skimming earthward. We thought things were going as planned and help had arrived, and was arriving all the time. We had also seen a C-47 crash in flames some distance from us, and I can still see it disappear behind yonder hill.

As we moved forward we came across parachute equipment: some loose; some in bundles still unopened; and a few opened with part of the load removed and part still there. From one bundle we took a bazooka and twelve rockets. We exchanged an M-1 rifle that had snapped at the stock on the jump for this bazooka.

Over more hedges and always bearing north we went, when all of a sudden we came upon two tents and two motorcycles. We found, after a close and careful investigation and on the alert for booby traps, that there was no one there, and that it was the C.P. of some officer of the German Army. We did no extensive damage to the contents of the tent because of possible booby traps, but we did puncture the tires of the two motorcycles, rendering them useless.

Across another field and another road we ran into one Lt. Harold V. Richard, "A" Co. 508th, and his communication Sergeant, Sergeant Hall. We were acquainted and were glad to have each others' company. After greetings and a conference we decided to ask directions at a large stone farmhouse about 50 yards away. We had 12 men now, including us two officers, so we split up and surrounded the house. Lt. Richard, one enlisted man, and I pounded on the door of the farmhouse. In a few minutes a very excited Frenchman came rushing—or gushing is more like it—out of the door. Several others were looking out of the windows on the ground floor, as well as from the windows on the other floors of the house.

By using our French guidebook and maps, we found that we were between Picauville and Etienville. We had a definite location to work on. We were about midway between the two places. In the house the upstairs windows were now alive with little kiddos wild eyed at seeing the American uniforms instead of the usual German ones.

Along came a car, and we decided to stop it. Lt. Richard moved out of the doorway towards the side of the house. The French occupants moved into the house and closed the door. Some of the paratroopers went to the sides of the house, and after the door was shut I went to the road and put up my hand and yelled 'STOP!' But the car just came faster. When it went by me I ran to the other side of the road, and I guess that we all fired at the car at the same time, as a dozen or more shots rang out. The car was hit, the windshield was shattered, and the driver crashed into the stone wall at the end of the house, and maybe into the side of the house before it came to a complete halt. When we got to the side of the road and attempted to stop it, it was not so easily done, as they increased their speed, and as I said, they crashed. There were holes all over the car: back, front, and sides. The chauffeur, a German Corporal, was trying to hide in a cellar window recess, and an officer was in the middle of the road, crawling towards the Luger pistol that had been knocked from his grasp as the car crashed into the stone and concrete house and wall. The third occupant of the car was not to be seen at the moment. The car was a Dusenberg or a Mercedes Phaeton. Later I learned that one Lt. Bush of the 82nd Division G-2 Section was using it for his transportation.

The corporal was still trying to get into the cellar and I shot him at him, but he was nearly covered by the ground and the entrance to the cellar window. He was wounded by my shot, being hit across the top of his left shoulder.

The Major (the man in the car) was killed as they tried to speed past us. The third German, as I said, was crawling towards his luger lying in the road, and all of the time that he was crawling he was looking up at me (I had crossed the road after the car went past me and climbed on a banking beside the road, four or five feet higher than the road, to get a good command of the situation. Thus I was above the corporal and my shots grazed his shoulder—the only part of him that was above the surface of the cellar window—and also four or five feet above the road where the General was crawling) and pleading in German and saying in English, 'Don't kill, don't kill!' I thought, I am not a cold hearted killer, I am human, but if he gets that Luger it's either him, one of my men, or me! So I shot! He was hit in the forehead and never knew it. He suffered none. The blood spurted from his forehead just like water from a fountain, and then it gradually subsided.

Upon examining the personnel that we had encountered we found that we had killed a Major, a Major General, and as a captive, a Corporal. We forced him to carry two briefcases found in the car full of papers and maps, as we took him along with us.

As we left the scene I tore the General's hat apart, looking for further identification of his name or the unit to which he was assigned, but I found only a name hand printed in it. The name was FALLEY...."

325th Glider Infantry Regiment

Company F, 3rd Battalion (Lt. Colonel Charles A. Carrell), supporting Company C, 746th Tank Battalion, landed on Utah Red Beach at 1400, de-waterproofed vehicles, and moved inland at 1600 to make contact with the Division. Two tanks were knocked out. The remainder of the regiment prepared to take off from airports in England.

82nd Airborne division Artillery

Parachute elements jumped at 0210 hours, joined a group from the 508th, and assisted in the attack on La Fiere Bridge. At 1330 hours this element joined the glider element at the Division CP. Glider elements landed at 0500 hours and moved directly to the Division CP. At 2305 hours Headquarters and Headquarters Battery of Division Artillery, the 319th Glider Field Artillery Battalion, and the 320th Glider Field Artillery Battalion glided into Normandy and encountered severe enemy small arms and mortar fire. Reorganization commenced immediately, but was handicapped by intense enemy fire. The section of the 456th Parachute Field Artillery Battalion attached to the 505th jumped with the 3rd Bn, but was able to assemble only one of the two 75mm pack howitzers that had been dropped.

80th Airborne Antiaircraft Battalion (AT)

Batteries A and B landed by glider at 0405. Six 57mm antitank guns had been recovered and were in position by 1730 hours. Battery C glided into the area at 2100 hours and began assembly and reorganization. The remainder of the Battalion sailed from Bristol, England, at 0645 hours.

307th Airborne Engineer Battalion

Company B (less one platoon attached to the 505th) jumped with the 508th at 0210 hours. Some Engineer personnel took up a defensive position at La Fiere in support of one group of the 508th, while other personnel joined the 508th group west of the Merderet River. One stick, which included the Battalion Commander, was dropped over Saint Sauveur Le Vicomte, and only a few escaped. Part of Headquarters and Company A landed by glider at 2300 hours and started to assemble under heavy enemy artillery and small arms fire. The remainder of the Battalion prepared to take off from airports in England.

307th Airborne Medical Company

Elements of the company landed by glider about 2100 and immediately began assemble, recovering by use of life rafts much equipment from gliders that had landed in shallow water near the banks of the Merderet River. A clearing station was set up at a crossroad north of Blosville.

82nd Airborne Signal Company

Parachute and glider elements of the company that landed prior to H-Hour were scattered and assembled with difficulty. Much equipment was lost. Only one of the three SCR 193 radios that landed during D-Day was operative, and it was not until the night of June 6-7 that radio contact was established with the 4th Infantry Division, or with the Division base in England.

D plus 1, 7 June 1944

The Division continued to assemble, reorganize, and secure its area against extremely severe enemy resistance, which included armor. Enemy troops, identified as the 91st Infantry Division (General Wilhem Falley), were held along the Merderet River to the west and were driven back to the north and northwest. Contact was established with the 4th infantry Division during the day, and the VII Corps Commander visiting the Division Command Post late in the day. The 325th GIR arrived by glider during the morning. Additional personnel that had been scatered in the original landings continued to report back to their units.

During the afternoon garbled radio messages signed "CO 507" were received at the Division Command Post, and it was finally determined that they originated with the Regimental Commander, Colonel Millett, who was isolated with a group of about 300 men west of Amfreville.

Captain Paul F. SMITH, "F" Co, 507th PIR

"In June 1944 I was in command of Company "F", 507th PIR, which in turn was attached to the 82nd airborne division. On 5 June at approximately 2330 "F" Co, as part of the 507th, took off in nine C-47 aircraft from the Barkston-Heath airfield in England, bound for a drop zone located approximately 900 yards north of Amfreville, Normandy. As part of the 2nd Battalion we were well back in the formation. I flew in the lead "F" Co plane with part of the company headquarters personnel, the battalion executive officer, major Ben Pearson, and one of the Regimental Chaplains. It was a clear night, and takeoffs were accomplished without incident. The formation was fine until we reached the west coast of the Normandy Peninsula, at which point we ran into a low, dense cloud bank that caused the sky train formation to break up. A few minutes after passing the coastline, as I looked out the aircraft astro-dome I could see only one other plane. Shortly thereafter I hooked up my stick and stood in the door waiting for the green light. We ran out of the cloud formation, whereupon I could see the ground and recognized my final ground checkpoint, the Douve River, running north-south. A few seconds after passing the river the left wing dipped, indicating a left turn. I watched for the green light, and when it did not come on decided that it was time to get out. I gave the command "GO" and promptly exited the plane. It was 0232 hours, June 6, 1944.

I landed in a field beside a road, and after getting out my harness, started down the line of flight to pick up the other members of my stick. At that point I could not identify my location on my map. I looked from then until well after daylight before finally running into a small group of men led by Major Pearson. After making this contact we met a French farmer walking along the road. He told us that we were only a short distance from the village of Le Ham. We then determined that we actually were about 4000 yards north of our designated drop zone. With Major Pearson in command of the group we started for our initial objective, the town of Amfreville, picking up a few more men on the way. In the meantime, my radio operator was busy trying to contact other elements of the battalion, without succes. Major Pearson told him to switch to the regimental frequency in an attempt to establish contact with regimental headquarters. This was done, and a short time later we were in contact with the regimental commander, Colonel George V. Millett, who directed Major Pearson to lead the group to the location of the regimental command post (CP). I did not hear the conversation, but a short time later Major Pearson told me about it, and also told me that Col. Millett had given him (Major Pearson) the coordinates of the CP. We moved all that day (D-Day), picking up small groups of parachutists and engaging in several firefights with the Germans, but never locating the CP.

Late that afternoon major Pearson again contacted Col. Millett, obtaining from him a new location of the regimental CP, and immediately after dark we started out again. We moved west all night without locating any American troops. At daylight we found ourselves west of the Gourbesville-Etienville highway. At this time I called Col. Millett and asked him for his location, reporting ours at the same time. He gave me the coodinates of his position and told me that he would send a guide to meet us. We moved off again, this time heading east, and a short time later ran into 1st Sgt. Barney Hopkins at the southeast corner of the woods. He told us he was the guide sent out by Col. Millett and promptly led the way to our regimental CP. Here we found Col. Millett, a Lt. Col. from another parachute regiment, several other officers from the 507th, and about 120 enlisted men. We stayed in that position under constant attacks all that day and night. The next morning Capt. Taylor, company commander of "H" Co, arrived with several more officers and about 100 men. By this time available ammunition was very low, and we were without food, except for a small amount taken from a German truck captured the previous day. It was now the morning of D+2, and the attacks against our thinly held positions were increasing in intensity. We held the position all that day, but when darkness fell preparations were made to move out. Up to that time I had not been informed of Col. Millett's plans, nor to my knowledge had any of the other officers. I made inquiries of Major Pearson as to what our mission was and where we were going. He told me that Col. Millett had finally contacted Division and been told to go to the Merderet River to make contact with another group of Americans under the command of a Lt. Col. Shanley. Shortly before midnight several tanks or self-propelled artillery pieces moved into position to our west and north, and Col. Millett decided we had better get moving. Just after midnight, by the light of a house set afire by the Germans, our force got underway, with Col; Millett and Capt. Taylor leading the way and Lt. Roger Whiting and I acting as the rear guard element. We were approximately 250 Americans with 96 prisoners to take along and guard. The column moved out of the south end of the CP area and turned northeast toward the Amfreville-Gourbesville highway. A short time later, as Lt. Whiting and I were patrolling the prisoner column, we heard two MG42s firing up ahead. We moved to the head of the column, where I talked to Col. Millett. He told me that he was gonig to backtrack the column and try another route. I told him that Whiting and I would stay in place to cover the column while it backed itself. As the column moved back Lt. Whiting and I threw hand grenades and fired at the MG42s, distracting the attention of the gunners until the column was clear of the area. We then backtracked and eventually caught up to the column, which was halted. We moved up the column to the location of the prisoners and sat down to rest. When the column hadn't moved in about fifteen minutes we suspected something was wrong. We moved toward the head of the column but found that the front half of the column had moved off—a connecting file had fallen asleep. We now were located west of the Amfreville-Gourbesville highway.

Suddenly I found myself in command of about 150 men and 90-some prisoners, with only a vague idea of where we were supposed to be going and of our mission when we got there. I did know, however, that Col. Millett originally was headed in the direction of the Merderet River, which was located to our east, so I decided to keep on in that direction. We crossed the highway and shortly therafter met Capt. Frank, a 507th officer who had been with the Col. Millett group. He said that he had missed the rear half of the column and had turned back to locate us. He thought he knew where the front part of the column was located and proceeded to guide us forward to the east and slightly north until daylight overtook us in a large square field, from which we could see the Merderet River. I decided to take up a perimeter defense of this area until we could locate the friendly troops with whom we were to make contact. Before we could occupy the entire perimeter we received intense small arms fire from the northern and eastern edges of the field. I gave orders to withdraw to the southeast, keeping parallel to the river. Shortly after leaving that field we encountered a small settlement of houses from which we received heavy small arms and machine gun fire. I decided our best course was to go through the settlement and clear it of Germans, and gave orders to that effect. This firefight lasted an hour or so, with about ten percent casualties for our forces, some of which were inflicted by artillery and mortar fire that began falling in the settlement just as we routed the last of the Germans. After cleaning out this settlement we proceeded south toward the sound of firing, which I felt sure marked the area for which we were looking. When we had gone about 600 yards southeast of the settlement, I decided we had better halt and orgonize ourselves into a tactical force capable of being maneuvered, to count noses, and to send out patrols to try to find Colonel Millett and any other U.S. forces in the area. Accordingly, we halted and took up defensive positions around a field. I began the task of organizing our force and simultaneously attempted to reach regimental headquarters by radio (we had one 300 radio with very weak batteries). First Sgt. Hopkins, with the aid of prisoners, was attempting to salvage parachute bundles lying in the swamp bordering the river. Some of the bundles had been booby-trapped, causing the loss of several prisoners, while several more prisoners were lost to German machine gun fire coming from both up and downriver on our side. About this time I managed to reach Regiment on the emergency channel and talked to Lt.Col. Arthur Maloney, acting Regimental Commander in the absence of Col. Millett. I reported our position and the number of personnel available and asked for orders. A few minutes later he told me to stay where I was until further orders from him. Immediately after I terminated that conversation with Lt. Col. Maloney, the Lt. Col. who had been with Col. Millett walked into our perimeter with about 25 or 30 men. He told me that all of the remainder of the original front half of the column, including Col. Millett and Major Pearson, had been captured that morning. He told me also that they (meaning he and the men accompanying him) had seen a large body of Germans headed our way, and that our only hope of survival was to cross the Merderet River to join friendly troops on the other side. I argued vehemently against such a course of action for several reasons, which I enumerated for him. First of all, I had orders to remain where I was until further orders from my acting regimental commander. Second, we had our backs to the swamp and river, thereby having to defend only three sides of our perimeter. And I believed we could successfully defend ourselves against a fairly large force. Third, we could hear the sound of an engagement going on to the southwest, indicating that there were other U.S. troops on our side of the river. I felt that in all probality they comprised the force with which we were to have made contact. Fourth, the Merderet was in flood stage, thereby flooding the countryside so that, at the point where we would have to cross, it was approximately 1100 yards wide. Most of this was swamp and could be negotiated, but the Germans had visual command of this particular stretch of river and could annihilate our group as it attempted to cross. I told the Lt. Col. that if he wanted to take the group with which he arrived, less any 507 people, across the river, I would have no issue with his decision. He refused to take any cognizance of my arguments and informed me that as senior officer present he was taking command of the force, and for me to get 4 or 5 men and lead the way across the river. I told him that I would accede to his order only under protest, and that I wanted the order repeated in the presence of two witnesses of my choosing. He agreed and repeated the order in the presence of Lt. Horace Cofer and 1st Sgt. Barney Hopkins. I then picked 5 men, among them 1st Sgt Hopkins, and we started across. We received machine gun fire, but none of the U.S. personnel was hit, although we did lose several prisoners to the fire. We crossed the railroad at a small station house, where I posted Lt. John Joseph and Lt. Cofer to direct the men as they arrived. We reached dry ground, where we encountered several members of the 505th PIR. When all were across and on dry land I had 1st Sgt. Hopkins count heads, and we established a defensive position. The Lt. Col. left for the Division CP. I notified Lt. Col. Maloney of our new location and then took our prisoners (now dwindled to 26) and our wounded to the Division POW enclosure and the 505th aid station, respectively. We stayed in that position through the night, and early the next morning headed for the 507th area just south of La Fiere Bridge..."

325th Glider Infantry Regiment

The first glider elements began landing at 0700 hours about 2,500 yards southeast of Sainte Mere Eglise. There were many crash landings, and casualties totalled approximately 7.5 per cent. Assembly was rapid, however, and by 1015 hours all battalions had reported. The 3rd Battalion moved out toward Carquebut at 1415 hours and reached Le Port without encountering opposition. The remainder of the regiment proceeded to move into an assembly area northeast of Chef du Pont. At 1600 hours the 2nd Battalion (Lt. Colonel John H. Swenson) was ordered to move into an assembly area east of La Fiere, and later was attached to the 505th at 2100 hours. The 1st (Lt. Colonel Klemm R. Boyd) and 3rd Bn (Lt. Colonel Charles A. Carrell) were ordered to move into and to outpost the regimental assembly area. Company F, 3rd Bn, in support of Company C, 746th Tank Bn, and 1st platoon, troop B, 4th Cavalry Reconnaissance Squadron, assisted the 8th Infantry in its attack toward Sainte Mere Eglise from the west at 0630 hours and made contact with gliderborne elements of the 325th by 0900. The 325th's regimental strength at the close of the day was approximately 85 per cent.

S.R Hartline, 325th Glider Infantry Regiment

"...We had been sealed in camp at Camp Williams, a marshalling area and airfield fifteen miles northeast of Exeter. The airfield was called Uppottery, taking its name from the nearby Devonshire village.

The days before June 5th were spent doing the usual training, and being issued our equipment and rations we would need on landing.

On June 5th we took part in studying maps of our landing and sand table models. After lunch and toward evening we watched the paratroopers loading up. It took the planes some time to form up after they had taken off. We went to bed and tried to get some sleep, which was to hard to do, realizing that the planes that would return would soon be pulling us in the gliders

On June 6th the paratroopers had been dropped and were meeting stiff resistance; and the order was received to commit the 325th GIR.

The planes had returned, were checked over, and cleared to tow us in. The glider we would use was checked over and cleared to carry us. The glider was the CG-4A, which carried thirteen men, or a jeep and four-man crew, and two pilots. Many of this type glider were made at the Ford Plant in Kingsford. The other was a much larger British glider, made of Plywood and carrying 28 troops and two pilots.

The glider used in the war was much different than the sailplanes you see in use today. Some people refer to the ones used in the war as Silent Wings; they did not make much noise but could not glide. They had to cut loose very near to the landing zone. The C-47s towing them made a lot of noise.

My Company was assigned to the Horsa's. On D+1 June 7th we were awakened at 0230 hours and given a quick breakfast a half an hour later. We returned to our tents and hastily secured our equipment.

We were formed in our platoons and marched to the airfield and the glider we were to ride in. Our glider was near the end of the formation, so we knew we would be some of the last to land.

We had a pretty good wait. Some of the conversation was about riding in "flying coffins," "tow targets," or "flak hacks," as the gliders were so often called. One Gliderman wanted to know whether this trip was really necessary.

As the C-47s began warming up we were ordered to load the glider. Everyone was assigned a seat. Our platoon leader, 2nd Lt. Robert Maxwell, had the first seat on the right, behind the pilots. My seat was the first seat on the left. The portion my seat was attached to was reinforced, and could be lowered down to drive the Jeeps in for loading. There was a wall between the pilots and cargo space.

We were airborne around 0630 AM. It took some time to get into formation and head toward France. We were escorted mostly by P-38s and British Spitfires. The Luftwaffe never made an appearance, and flak was almost absent. We could look down and see ships in every direction for as far as you could see.

After we passed over the coast I awakened Lt. Maxwell and told him we were over land. He stood up and was standing in the doorway between the pilots. We flew about five or six miles inland to near Chef du pont, where our landing zone was. The larger field we were to land in was found to have been posted with large posts. This made it necessary for us to land in the smalller fields. Since we were in a glider near the end of the formation we didn't have much choice of fields.

The glider was cut loose and we landed, but the field was slightly slanted. The pilot put on full brakes and full flaps. Due to the grass being wet from the dew it seemed like we gained speed. I think the pilot was trying to steer the glider between two large trees in the hedgerow, but our right wing caught the wing of a glider that had already hit the hedgerow. Lt. Maxwell was still standing in the doorway and was killed at impact.

I had tightened my seat belt as tight as I could, put the butt of my rifle against the inside of my right foot, and held the muzzle end of the rifle as hard as I could diagonally across my body toward the front of the glider, hoping this would clear the petition between me and the pilot out of the way. It must have done the job, for I was still holding it that way when I came to on the other side of the hedgerow.

The pilot was still living, so I gave him a shot of morphine. The co-pilot and the first eight on the right were killed.

Only 37 men out of a company of 128 were accounted for. After the landing we were ordered to assemble and passed through Chef Du Pont. We made no contact with the enemy, for we had landed in the forward lines of the 4th Division. They had received light resistance on Utah Beach. We formed a bivouac in a orchard for supper...."

505th Parachute Infantry Regiment

The 2nd and 3rd Battalions (Lt. Col. Vandervoort and Lt. Col. Krauze) continued to hold Sainte Mere Eglise against severe attacks from the north and south. The 2nd Battalion patrols contacted elements of the 8th Infantry Regiment of the 4th ID at Saint Martin at 1000 hours and attacked north to clear the outskirts of Sainte Mere Eglise. The 1st Battalion (Lt. Colonel frederick Kellam) withstood several counterattacks and pushed the enemy back to the eastern bank of the Merderet River, in the vicinity of La Fiere Bridge. They were supported late in the day by one platoon of tanks from Company C, 746th Tank Battalion. At the close of the period the 2nd and 3rd Battalions prepared to attack north toward Neuville Au Plain in conjunction with the 4th ID's drive on the right. The 2nd Battalion, 325th GIR, was attached at 2100 to assist in this attack.

Marcus Heim, "A" Co, 505th PIR

"...A little after migdnight on June 6, 1944, I jumped out of a C-47 airplane over Normandy, France, with the 82nd Airborne Division. The objective of the 82nd was the crossroads of the town of Sainte Mere Eglise and the Merderet and Douve River valleys. I was with "A" Company, 505th PIR, and our objective was La Fiere Bridge, over the Merderet River.

I landed about 25 feet from a road, and before I could get my rifle assembled I heard a motorcycle approaching. I remained still, as I did not have time to assemble my rifle, and watched two German soldiers pass by. After they passed I had my rifle together, and I found other paratroopers and our equipment bundle and set off for the bridge over the Merderet River. We were to hold the bridge until the soldiers who landed on the beach arrived later that day, but it was three days before they reached our position.

As you stand at the La Fiere Bridge looking in the direction of Sainte Mere Eglise, the Manor house is on the right and was the living quarters. There were several buildings, one a large barn that was close to the Merderet River.

The Germans had occupied the Manor House and were driven out by "A" Co, 505th, after heavy fighting. As you pass the Manor house toward Sainte Mere Eglise the road goes uphill and curves to the left. Across from the Manor house there was a pathway that was about four feet wide, and now is a paved road about seven feet wide. As you look across the bridge toward Cauquigny, the causeway was narrow and had brush and trees on each side, some hanging over the causeway. The fields were completely flooded right up to the causeway. The town of Cauquigny was about 800 to 900 yards from the bridge, and it was in German hands. The causeway curved to the right about 60 or 65 yards from the bridge.

When we arrived at the bridge, men were placed down the pathway to the right and to the left of the Manor House and out buildings. The four bazooka men (Lenord Peterson and myself, John Bolderson, and Gordon Pryne) were given our positions. We (Peterson and I) were deployed on the Manor House side facing Cauquigny, below the driveway. There was a telephone pole just in front of us and we dug in behind it. We knew that when the Germans started the attack with their tanks we would have to get out of our foxhole and reveal our position so we could get a better view of the tanks. Bolderson and Pryne were on the right side of the road just below the pathway. I do not remember how many paratroopers were around us, all I saw was a machine gun set up in the Manor House yard. On the right side down the pathway a few riflemen were placed. There was a 57mm cannon up the road in back of us, along with another machine gun. We carried antitank mines and bazooka rockets from the landing area. These mines were placed across the causeway, about 50 or 60 feet on the other side of the bridge. There was a broken down German truck by the Manor House that we pushed and dragged across the bridge placed across the causeway. All that afternoon the Germans kept shelling our position, and the rumor was that the Germans were going to counter attack. Around 0500 hours in the afternoon the Germans started the attack; two tanks with infantrymen on each side, and in the rear following them was a third tank with more infantry following it. As the lead tank started around the curve in the road the tank commander stood up in the turret to take a look, and from our left the machine gun let loose a burst and killed the commander. At the same time the bazookas, 57mm, and everything else we had were firing at the Germans, and they in turn were shooting at us with cannon, mortars, machine guns, and rifle fire. Lenord Peterson and myself, the loader, in the forward position got out of the foxehole and stood behind the telephone pole so we could get a better shot at the tanks. We had to hold our fire until the last minute because some of the tree branches along the causeway were blocking our view. The first tank was hit and started to turn sideways, and at the same time was swinging the turret around and firing at us. We had just moved forward around the cement telephone pole when a German shell hit and we had to jump out of the way to avoid being hit as it was filling. I was hoping that Bolderson and Pryne were also firing at the tanks, for with all that was happening in front of us there was no time to look around to see what others were doing. We (Peterson and I) kept firing at the first tank until it was put out of action and on fire. The second tank came up and pushed the first tank out of the way. We moved forward toward the second tank and fired at it as fast as I could load the rockets in the bazooka. We kept firing at the second tank, and we hit it in the turret where it is connected to the body, in the track, and with another hit it went up in flames. We were almost out of rockets and the third tank was still moving. Peterson asked me to go back across the road and see if Bolderson had any extra rockets. I ran across the road, and with all the crossfire I still find it hard to believe I made to the other side in one piece. When I got to the other side I found one dead soldier and Bolderson and Pryne were gone. Their bazooka was lying on the ground, and it was damaged by what I thought were bullet holes. Not finding Bolderson or Pryne, I presumed that either one or both were injured. I found the rockets they left, and then had to return across the road to where I left Peterson. The Germans were still firing at us, and I was lucky again, as I returned without being hit. Peterson and I, with the new found rockets, put these to use on the third tank. After that one was put out of action the Germans pulled back to Cauquigny and continued shelling us for the rest of the night. They tried two other counter attacks on our position that also failed.

During the battles one does not have time to look around to see how others are doing. We were told that when we took up our position by the bridge that we had to hold it at all cost until the men from the beaches arrived, for if the Germans broke through they would have a good chance of going all the way to the beach. Our job (Peterson and I) was to be in the forward position by the La Fiere Bridge with our bazooka to stop any German tanks from advancing over the bridge and onto Ste Mere Eglise and the beaches. This we accomplished, while all the while the Germans were continuously firing everything they had at us. After I went across the road and found more rockets for the bazooka and returned the third tank was put out of action and the Germans retreated, and we (Peterson and I) were just on our side of the bridge. When the Germans pulled back we looked around; we did not see anyone, so we moved back to our foxhole. Looking back up the road toward Ste Mere Eglise we saw that the 57mm gun and the machine gun were destroyed. Looking down the pathway across from the Manor House we could not see any of our men. We were thinking that we were all alone, and that maybe we should move from there, but then someone came and told us to hold our position; they would find more men to place around us, for the Germans may try again to breach our lines. We found out later that of the few that were holding the bridge at this time, most were either killed or wounded. Why we were not injured or killed only the good Lord knows. (Author's Note: For holding their position and repelling the Germans that day, June 6, 1944, Marcus Heim and Lenord Pryne were awarded the Distinguished Service Cross, which is the second highest award in the United States. However, of the men who survived and were up on the hill and could see most of the action they believed these men should have received the Congressional Medal of Honor."

507th Parachute Infantry Regiment

The regiment moved into an area west of Sainte Mere Eglise and rested and reorganized. At 1600 hours the regiment moved into positions south of the La Fiere - Sainte Mere Eglise road west of the railroad to assist the 1st Bn, 505th, against a threatened countreattack at the La Fiere Bridge. At 1900 hours the 507th, at approximately 25 per cent strenght, successfully pushed the enemy back to the west bank of the Merderet River in its sector.

Captain Roy Creek, "E" Co, 507th PIR

"... Troopers kept drifting in, and our force was growing. Men came from all units of the 82nd Airborne Division, and some from the 101st Airborne. Nothing of consequence happened, and soon it was dawn. We know nothing of what had happened to anyone outside our own small group. There was no tactical unity and no supporting weapons, just a group of invaders who were wondering what had happened to all of their thorough planning. Just before daybreak the first gliders began to come in. One landed in a flooded area about 150 yards from where we had our perimeter set up. As the men started to come out of the glider, enemy machine gun fire opened up from the hedgerow on the other side. Men coming out of the glider were being hit. Fire was placed in the general vicinity of the machine gun, and this enabled a few men to make the hedgerow, behind which we had cover.

About 0900 hours Lt.Col. Ostberg, Commander 1st Battalion 50Ëth PIR, returned from the Command Post of Gen. Gavin and informed us that General Gavin was moving toward La Fiere and that we were to follow. This meant fording the flooded area that we had already struggled through earlier in the day. We pulled out of our position, leaving the wounded marked and as comfortable as possible, and started across the marsh. As we waded in water sometime chest deep we were fired on by snipers, who appeared to be firing from long range because of the inaccuracy of their fire. But one could not help being concerned about the shots splashing water in one's face. All that could be done was to keep on walking and hoping.

We made it to the other side without mishap. We marched south until we reached high ground overlooking the La Fiere Bridge. When we arrived, Gen. Gavin told us we should proceed south along the railroad to Chef-Du-Pont, where we were to seize the town and bridge across the Merderet, west of the center of town. A few men who had been able to get some automatic weapons from some of the bundles dropped as we jumped were attached for this mission, and under the command of Col. Ostberg we proceeded down the railroad toward Chef-Du-Pont. There were about 100 men altogether, equipped only with what they could carry: rrifles; submachine guns; three machine guns; and grenades of various types, including the British Gammon grenade, which packed a terrific wallop. At about 1000 6 June Col. Ostberg and his force, comprised of men of all units of the 507th and some from the 508th, had reached the railroad station of Chef-Du-Pont without any opposition. The railroad station was in the center of town, and the small but important bridge was a short distance southwest. A squad was sent to clear the section of town northeast of the station, which they did without incident. The remainder of the force led by Col. Ostberg started to race through the part of the town leading to the bridge. This group was fired upon from several buildings simultaneously. Four of the men were hit, and the remainder were forced to hold until the town could be systematically cleared. This took about two hours. By that time most of the Germans had withdrawn ahead of us, apparently headed for the bridge. Speed seemed to be the answer. We knew the bridge must be taken before the Germans could organize their defense, so we made a semi-organized dash for it. We were too late. Two officers reached the bridge and were both shot, one toppling off the bridge and into the water, the other officer falling on the eastern approach. The officer toppling into the river was Col. Ostberg. He was rescued shortly afterward by two soldiers of the 507th and lived to fight again. The other officer was dead. A short time later Col. Maloney arrived with about 75 more men, and we set about dislodging the stubborn enemy.

The railroad split the town, and the bridge lay to the south and west of the railroad station. Houses lined both sides of the road leading to the bridge. A short distance from the bridge on the left side of the road leading to the bridge was a large creamery that was two stories high, and afforded good observation from an upstairs window. South of the creamery and on three sides of the bridge there were obstacles—flooded areas. For pratical purposes, the only approach to the bridge was the one we had chosen through Chef-Du-Pont. The approaches from the west were causeways, long and straight, and completely flooded on both sides. Germans were dug in on the shoulders on both sides of the road, occupying foxholes dispersed at intervals of about ten yards for a long stretch leading to the bridge and beyond. No one could hope to attack succesfully or withdraw along these causeways without a preponderance of supporting fires, which was something we did not have. Nevertheless, we were on the outskirts of Chef-du-Pont with 175 men. What are we waiting for? Let's take the bridge. Two attempts to storm the bridge proved unsuccessful. There had to be a better way. We did succeed in clearing the eastern side of the bridge, however, by overrunning the position along the shoulders of the road.

Our own position along the edge of the road east of the bridge had become almost untenable because of rifle and direct artillery fire coming from our right flank. Just as it was beginning to look as though we might have a stalemate, Col. Maloney was called back to La Fiere with all men available, leaving only about 34 men at Chef-du-Pont. Concurrent with his departure three things happened: one, direct artillery fire on our positions around the creamery reduced our strength to 20 men; two, an observation point in the creamery noted what was estimated to be a company of Germans moving around to our left rear (This threat never materialized, for they by-passed us in route to Ste Mere Eglise where, though not known to us at the time, a battle was being waged by elements of the 505th for that important objective); and three, an officer delivered a message from Gen. Gavin, "hold at all costs." It was pretty obvious that it could not cost much more, but at the same time, it was doubtful we could hold something we did not have. Reinforcements were requested, and as from heaven C-47s began to appear, dropping bundles of weapons and ammunitions. One bundle of 60mm mortar ammunition dropped right in our laps. Within 30 minutes the officer who had previously delivered the "hold at all costs" message returned with 100 men and a 57mm gun, which was pulled into position on our side of the bridge. We started firing at the enemy field piece. I am sure we did not hit it, but we stopped the firing, and that is what we had to do in order to survive.

At the beginning of this period of heavy shelling I found myself exposed with no place to go. I spotted a very small brick sentry house just short of the bridge on our side. I made a dash for it, went inside, and found a still burning enemy soldier, a victim of a white phosphorous grenade that apparently had been tossed in on him during earlier fighting. The house only had room for one man standing, so it became crowded with my arrival, and the other guy in there was not going anywhere. This, coupled with the fact that the smoke and strench from the burning man, caused me to make a quick decision that I would rather take my chances out in the open than risk the consequences of smoke inhalation. Besides, I reasoned that this lone house was surely an aiming point for the artillery. With our reinforcements, strong positions were organizated to our rear and along the flooded area on either side of the road and east of the bridge. The defenses were tied in with natural obstacles on three sides of us. We opened fire with every weapon we could get into position, including our 60mm mortar. On a prearranged signal, all fires lifted and ten men and one officer stormed the bridge and went into position on the western approach to guard the causeway. Five Germans made a run for it down the deathtrap causeway and were immediately shot down. That did it. The battle was over."

508th Parachute Infantry Regiment

Colonel Louis G. Mendez, 3rd Bn, 508th PIR

"...I was in command of the 3rd Bn at the outset. We ran into a lot of trouble as soon as we hit land. The flak was terrific. We jumped from about 2100 feet—the entire serial—and were going rather fast. 2100 feet is too much of a ride; I checked my field bag and found 3 bullet holes in it. Lt. Daly was subsecuently killed. I landed about 0230 in the morning and did not see anybody for five days, with the possible exception of my messenger. I batted 1000 with my pistol; I got three Heines with three shots, two Heines with a carbine, and one Heine with a hand grenade. The Germans had a very good means of communication. We seemed to run into antiparatroop groups of about 60 men, and we shot back and forth. We concluded that these groups called other groups who were waiting for us. Altogether I had three men, one officer and my messenger. The most outstanding thing I learned was the accurate intelligence of the Germans. They used full names, even nicknames to confuse my company commanders. My company commanders stated that they received messages in my full name and even my nickname. It is essential that the challenging system must be known to the air Corps as well, in case they end up on the ground. The reply to the challenge must be given very quickly, or it will be too bad.

We landed about 1/2 a mile from the DZ, southeast. It was on the north side of the Douve River. In the five days that I was separeted from the battalion I walked 90 miles. I was looking for the 2nd Bn, and all I found was ack-ack. We never saw a T, we jumped on the green light. The pilot did not see the T light either...."

One group near the railroad moved into positions in the vicinity of the road junction at Chef du Pont to protect the Division's north flank against enemy penetration. This group was in position by 0630 hours, but it later moved to join another group of the regiment in position defending the Chef du Pont Bridge. It mopped up numerous enemy strong points surrounding Chef du Pont, and established patrol contact with elements of the regiment west of the Merderet River on the high ground. The group on the high ground, now reorganized as the 2nd Battalion (Major Thomas Shanley), had completed organization of its position by 1300 hours, wiping out a number of enemy mortar and artillery positions. A roadblock was set up on the western approaches to the Chef du Pont Bridge, and contact was established with forces in Chef du Pont. Regimental strength at the close of the day was approximately 25 per cent.

Irwing Shanley, 2nd Bn, 508th PIR

On the jump into Normandy Pfc Shanley landed in a tall tree in a hedgerow and had to cut himself down with the trench knife strapped to his leg. He was momentarily stunned from the fall of about 15 feet into the hedgerow ditch, but recovered in time to challenge and be challenged by the trooper who followed him out of the aircraft, Pfc Alton H. Webster. Moments later they were joined by Pfc. Joseph Demarais. These three mortar platoon members then joined up with 14 other troopers from their battalion, and several hours after the drop joined up with a much larger force commanded by Lt. Colonel Thomas J.B. Shanley, their battalion commander.

The senior man in the 17-man group was a staff sergeant from "D" Co of the 2nd Bn, and he took charge of the group. The sergeant said that since the rest of the battalion was lost we should head for the causeway across the Douve River, which was one of the two bridges the regiment was to destroy. As they headed toward the causeway with the three mortarmen serving as point men, the 17-man group passed through a deserted enemy bivouac area, and a short time later came under heavy automatic weapons fire as it attempted to exit a pasture onto a small road near a large farmhouse in Picauville. Webster was shot in the chest from the initial burst, and the group withdrew to find another route to the causeway. Shanley and Desmarais helped Webster back away from the road and the enemy fire. They moved him to a safer spot and went back to the group, which was still moving away from the enemy fire, to get the medic who was with the group. Shanley, Desmarais, and the medic returned to Webster, and the medic administratered first aid as best he could under the circumstances. They reluctantly left Webster, who was severely wounded, to return to the group.

Irving Shanley continued to serve with the 2nd Battalion during the assault on Baupte and on Hill 131 until he was slightly wounded and evacuated to a field hospital. He was at the field hospital for three days and then returned to his unit for duty.

82nd Airborne Division Artillery

Various groups of artillery were involved in individual skirmishes with the enemy as they found their way back to their parent units. The 319th Glider Field Artillery Bn assembled east of Sainte Mere Eglise with six 75mm pack howitzers. The 320th Glider Field Artillery Bn was placed in direct support of the 505th. After salvaging two 105mm howitzers and taking over the 75mm pack howitzer of the 456th Parachute Field Artillery Bn detachment with the 505th, the 320th went into position 400 yards west of Sainte Mere Eglise. The first round was fired at 0911 hours. The seaborne echelon of the 456th PFA Bn arrived off Utah Beach but did not land.

80th Airborne Antiaircraft Battalion

Batteries A, B, and C continued to reorganize, and by 1800 hours six 57mm antitank guns of Battery C and three guns each from Batteries A and B were in position covering the two bridges over the Merderet River. The remainder of the Battalion remained on board ships preparing to disembark on Utah Beach.

307th Airborne Engineer Battalion

The remainder of Company A landed by glider at 0700 hours and moved to join the 325th GIR in the vicinity of Chef du Pont at 0930 hours. Bridges and culverts south of Le port and near Liesville were blown.

Aerial Resupply

An aerial resupply mission, including 148 of the 248 C-47 planes that had taken off, arrived over the area at 0620. They dropped 155.5 tons of ordnance, quartermasters, and medical supplies—74% of the originally scheduled load. The drop pattern was poor and bundles were scattered, many of them falling into enemy hands or being covered by enemy fire. Limited recovery was effected initially.

D plus 2, 8 June 1944

The Division continued to attack along its north flank, maintained its positions along the Merderet River, and cleared the southern flank area to establish contact with the 101st Airborne Division.

During the night of 7-8 June a messenger from the isolated group east of Amfreville crossed the Merderet River on a sunken bridge northwest of La Fiere and reported to the Division Command Post. It was now evident that there were three isolated groups west of the Merderet River:

- A strong force of 2nd Battalion, 508th, on high ground in the vicinity of Geutteville.
- The 2nd Battalion, 507th, located north of Hameau Flaux.
- A force of approximately 425 men, most of them from the 507th, located west of Amfreville.

As the above situation became clear, the Division Commander developed a plan to relieve the isolated groups west of the Merderet, and to establish a clearcut bridgehead over the river. The 1st Battalion, 325th GIR, was to cross the Merderet River on the sunken bridge northwest of La Fiere, establish contact with the 2nd Battalion, 507th, and swing south to capture the western approaches to the La Fiere Bridge. The 507th force west of Amfreville was to attack to the east to contact the 1st Battalion 325th, and 2nd Battalion, 507th. The 2nd Bn, 508th, was to remain in place.

325th Glider Infantry Regiment

At 2330 the 1st Battalion crossed the Merderet River northwest of La Fiere by means of a sunken road and a railroad embankment against little enemy opposition to establish a bridgehead and contact the isolated forces of the 507th. At the close of the period the 1st Battalion had crossed the river successfully and was marching towards the western approaches to the La Fiere Bridge.

505th Parachute Infantry Regiment

The 1st Battalion initially remained in position north of La Fiere assisting the 507th PIR in guarding the Merderet River crosssing at that point. The 2nd and 3rd Battalions attacked abreast to the north and seized Neuville au Plain by 0430 hours against slight opposition. Supported by the 2nd platoon, Company C, 746th Tank Battalion, these two battalions continued their attack to the north and seized Grainville by 2300 hours. The 1st Battalion relieved the 3rd Battalion, the 3rd then taking up a reserve position southwest of Grainville. Attached to the 505th, the 2nd Battalion, 325th GIR, assumed defensive positions west of the town and prepared to attack to the north toward Fresville on the Division's north flank at the close of the period.

507th Parachute Infantry Regiment

One force of 175 men isolated since D-Day on the west bank of the Merderet River, north of Hameau Flaux, was still intact, but suffered from heavy enemy artillery, mortar, and small arms fire. It attempted unsuccessfully to cross the River to the east to rejoin the Regiment. Part of the 507th force west of Amfreville succeeded in joining the group east of the town, but another portion of the group, including the Regimental commander, Colonel Millett, was ambushed and taken prisoner. The portion of the 507th east of the Merderet continued to hold a line, maintaining contact with adjacent regiments.

> Major Gordon Smith, S-4, 507th PIR
>
> "...I was the jumpmaster of the lead plane of the final nine of the 507 serial. The pilot was a Major Thompson, who had graduated with me in 1938 from the University of Wisconsin. He was the squadrom CO. At our pilot-jumpmaster briefing he said 'Smitty, I will put you right in the center of your DZ!' This did not turn out to be an exact truth, but not too far off of the designated 507 DZ. Later in 1947 Tommie and I met at an officers' club in Panama one evening, and he told me that due to all the flak he did a 180 and flew in on another direction. That landed most of my stick on the DZ, but myself and the Sgt behind me landed on the other side of the Merderet River.

Sgt Harmon Walters and I rounded up 8 other troopers, none from my plane and not all from the 507th. Three of them had lost all of their equipment, as they were dropped in the river or water flooded areas. We crossed the Merderet on a bridge at La Gare. This was 4 to 5 kilometres northwest of Sainte Mere Eglise and 1 or so kilometers west of the village of Fresville. We were heading for Gourbesville, on the Amfreville. It was intended that I set up a Re-supply drop area in or near Amfreville. I was the 507th S-4 (Supply Officer). We got off the road after passing the flooded area and entered a small apple orchard on some high ground, at which time we were fired on. We made a dash for a hedgerow, and I was hit in the right arm and flank by a single shot. Just then three truck loads of Germans stopped on the road to our left, and I could see we could do little good there. After Walters and others cleaned my wounds I ordered them to get out of there as best they could. Later in 1945 I found that they back tracked and ended up with the troops at La Fiere. I attempted to crawl on my elbows toward a French house, but the Germans came and picked me up. Two of them carried me to the road and stopped a Frenchman with a horse drawn cart. I was held between the two on the rear of the cart, and we ended up at what I believe was the town of Gourbesville at a German Aid Station. This is where I had a most unusual experience.

The German spoke English. He had been captured in north Africa, and as a POW of the Allies he was able to treat some of his own wounded. He told me that because of the fine treatment he had had prior to his return to the German Army, on an exchange of medical personnel, he would take the best care of me that he could. He had already operated on a Cpl. from the 508th that had been taken. He had to amputate the trooper's left arm. He informed me that he had done it so that at a later date a prosthesis could be fitted without a problem because of the way he had performed the amputation. He operated on me, and I was placed in a bed. Later when I awoke I was aware of a German soldier seated on a bench to the left of me. The doctor came into the room and told me that this was the German soldier (a white Russian) who had shot me. Also, that he had brought me a German mess kit of barley stew and a bottle of red wine. I was told not to eat anything, but to drink the wine, as I had lost a lot of blood. So here I am taking a sip and then the soldier drinking. We handed the bottle back and forth until the wine was gone. I cannot describe the look on the face of the German who had shot me. This was sometime around 2 or 3 PM. Sometime about midnight the doctor asked if the corporal from the 508th and I would like to be evacuated or put in the cellar. I said cellar. The Doctor said they expected that our own troops would take the town early in the morning. My decision regarding the cellar was short lived. A shouting German Colonel came in telling them to put the 508th corporal and I in an ambulance. Fifteen hours later we arrived at a German hospital, where I stil don't know. Later I and Captain William Paty, who was from HawaÔi and commanded "A"Co in the 501st PIR (and was also wounded), were put on a bus with others. I was placed on the floor of the bus, as I was still on a stretcher. After being taken on and off the bus at several stops and over a period of several days, we ended up at an old French school that had been converted to a POW hospital in Rennes...."

508th Parachute Infantry Regiment

Attacking with two reinforced companies, the regiment cleared the area on the Division's south flank to include the towns of Le Port, Carquebut, and Eturville by 1920 hours, and established contact with the 101st airborne Division at a road junction north of Blosville. Resistance was severe, but 160 prisoners were taken. The 2nd Battalion, on the west bank of the Merederet River, repulsed several sharp enemy tank counterattacks directed at the western causeway to the Chef Du Pont Bridge. Contact with the Regiment on the east bank could not be maintained because of excessive enemy activities and observation.

Jack Schlegel, Hq&Hq Co, 3rd Bn, 508th PIR

"...Je suis Americain!" Schlegel announced in school French, which was effective enough to calm the fears of the startled Normans. The paratroopers were invited inside.

Using sign language, French, German, and Americanese, the troopers learned that they were near Picauville, and their hosts were Mr and Mrs Lecomte. The Lecomtes served bread and wine to the paratroopers as they sat around the dining table and planned their route. As a parting gesture, Jack Schlegel gave his paratrooper wings to Madame Lecomte as a remembrance.

Schlegel's men started on their journey to find other members of their company and battalion. About daylight, Schlegel's group came upon a bullet-ridded German staff car rammed up against a stone wall and two dead Germans in the road. One of the dead was General Wilhelm Falley, CO of the 91st german Infantry Division, who had been killed earlier by Lt. Malcolm Brannen. In examining the car, Schlegel found a package that contained a large swatiska banner, the command flag of Gen. Falley.

Approaching footsteps were heard. The troopers hid behind a stone wall and waited. The footsteps were those of other wandering paratroopers. Schlegel's group joined in with these men. Schlegel's group made a break through a hedgerow, then fled toward a barn. As they entered the barn door three jerries were trying to get out the same door. The paratroopers grabbed the Germans and pulled them back inside as prisoners.

While the prisoners were guarded in a small room, Schlegel slipped away to another part of the barn. He pulled up a loose board in the floor, stuffed his package with Falley's command flag under the floor, replaced the loose plank, and covered it with straw. With their German prisoners as insurance the troopers left the barn safely. After traveling a few hundred yards they came face to face with a German tank, which fired its big gun. A shell exploded just behind the group and wounded many. One of the prisoners, although bleeding from his wounds, jumped up and waved cease fire gestures to the tank commander. The insurance paid off. The tank commander decided to take prisoners rather than finish off the Americans. After capture, Schlegel and the others walked several miles to a chateau, where there were about 250 prisoners.

The next day they were loaded on 20 new unmarked German trucks with canvas covers. The trucks moved out on a main highway toward Saint LÙ. About noon Allied planes strafed the convoy of POWs. Schlegel estimated the damage at approximately 30 or 40 of our men killed and over 80 wounded. All of us pitched on to help with the dead and wounded. I remember moving three from my own company with the dead and placing Lt. Bodack with the wounded. He was hit with three 50 caliber shells in the spine and never walked again, but survived the war (among the survivors was Col. Millett of the 507th PIR and ranking officer of the POWs. The Germans had Col. Millett organize the survivors and march them on their way).

Jack Schlegel made hist first escape the day of the strafing, which was the first of three unsuccesful attemps. On his fourth attempt Schlegel was aided by Dr. Enzinger, a German doctor in the POW hospital at Rennes.

Schlegel's family had moved to the U.S. from Germany when he was seven years old. Since Jack could speak German he was selected to interpret for the German doctor.

Dr. Enzinger told Jack that Gen. Patton's tanks were near. Jack had been given a pass by the doctor to run errands to the hospital annex. On his next trip to the annex, Jack waited until dark and slipped out of the compound. Two days later Cpl. Schlegel contacted the American troops under general George Patton's command.

Gen. Patton had a drink of Johnny Walker black label with Schlegel and sent him on his way toward Utah Beach in a jeep driven by Major F. J. Cibulka (Patton's G-2). On the way the major stopped by the barn where Gen. Falley's flag was hidden. Jack found his prized souvenir just where he had left it. (Author's Note: In 1969 Schlegel visited Normandy with the C-47 Club and donated the flag to the Sainte Mere Eglise Museum.)

82nd Airborne Division Artillery

The 319th Glider Field Artillery Battalion moved seven 75mm pack howitzers into position east of Chef Du Pont in support of the 507th and 508th. The 320th Glider Field Artillery Battalions moved eight 105mm M3 howitzers into position west of Sainte Mere Eglise in direct support of the 505th and 325th. The 87th Field Artillery Battalion was relieved of attachment to the Division before it was in position to fire a shot in support of the 82nd Division's operations.

Seaborne Echelon

The seaborne echelon, Force "C," began landing at 1500 hours, and moved into a bivouac area preparatory to joining the rest of the Division. Troops included the 456th Parachute Field Artillery Battalion, Batteries D, E, and F of the 80th Airborne Antiaircraft Battalion, Headquarters Company of the 307th Airborne Engineer Battalion, and some attached troops and seaborne elements of units that had arrived by parachute and glider.

D plus 3, 9 June 1944

The Division gained a clear-cut bridgehead over the Merderet River, relieved two of the three isolated groups and some members of the third, and continued its attack to the northwest in the Le Ham sector.

325th Glider Infantry Regiment

The 1st Battalion continued to press forward to reach the western approaches of the La Fiere Bridge, but at 0400 hours was pinned down by heavy fire of all types at Cauquigny. Following a 15-minute artillery preparation, the 3rd Battalion attacked across the La Fiere Bridge at 1050 hours with two companies of the 507th (Captain Robert Rae) and supported by Company C, 746th Tank Battalion. A bridgehead was established despite heavy losses. Cauquigny was secured by 1530 hours, and the 3rd Battalion was linked up with the 1st Battalion, 325th, on the left and the 2nd Battalion, 507th, on the right. Only a small portion of the group west of Amfreville succeeded in reaching the lines. An enemy counterattack lasting from 1900 to 2100 was repulsed successively by the 3rd Battalion and the 507th.

505th Parachute Infantry Regiment

Grainville and the bridge over the Merderet River at the town were seized by 0100. The regiment attacked again at 0530 with 2nd Battalion on the left, 2nd Battalion, 325th GIR attached, on the right, and 1st Battalion following. The rigiment reached a line 300 yards south of the canal by 1200. The 2nd Battalion then moved through positions of the 2nd Battalion, 325th, and continued the attack with the left Battalion.

507th Parachute Infantry Regiment

Two companies attacked across the La Fiere Bridge with the 325th GIR at 1030 to establish a firm bridgehead in a fierce and savage attack. These two companies captured Le Motey despite heavy fire of all types. Contact was made with the 2nd Battalion, 507th, and the two companies moved into a reserve position 500 yards east of Le Motey. The regiment again assisted the 325th at 2000 hours in repelling a strong enemy counterattack, the repulse of which assured a firm hold on the Merederet Bridgehead.

Captain Robert Rae, Service Co, 507th PIR

"...I landed in a small area right behind a large farmhouse. I had a feeling we were several miles away from our objective. The farmhouse had a shed in the backyard, and there were trees all around me. As soon as I hit the ground I heard fire several times, but on the third or fourth pass I realized it was just harassing fire and was not being aimed directly at me. Meanwhile, I was able to gather up about eight other boys. At the time I was a Captain in the service Company. We moved toward the farmhouse and started cleaning out the Germans inside. I remember about three or four Germans escaped out the back door.

We left the farmhouse and started moving down the road; we ran into a Frenchman, who was startled to see us. We tried to ask him where we were. We did not have much luck communicating with him, so I pulled out my map and he pointed to where we were. We were in the 101st drop zone. I knew where the 101st Airborne Division CP was supposed to be stationed, so we made our way the CP.

When we got to the CP I found the highest ranking officer I could find, identified myself, and asked him if I could take all the 82nd men that were in the CP and move towards our objective (Ste Mere Eglise). He agreed, so we gathered up the men—around 90—got on the road, and headed off towards Ste Mere Eglise. When I got into Ste Mere Eglise I reported to Lt. Col. Maloney, Executive Officer of the 507th PIR. Maloney told me to take up positions alongside the 505th. The 505th courageously held their positions against several German attacks across the La Fiere bridge causeway spanning the Merderet River.

Col. Maloney determined he had enough 507th personnel for three composite companies that he identified as Creek Co, Brackoneck Co, and Rae Co.

We made our way down towards the manorhouse by the bridge, and artillery shells were coming down very heavily. I reported to General Gavin, and he told me he wanted my men to be stationed near the 505th. We stayed there for about two days.

On the morning of D+3 we began to prepare for the attack. At about 1000 our artillery started firing. We were supposed to receive smoke, but we didn't get any. A full-strength battalion of the 325th GIR was to lead the attack across the bridge and establish a bridgehead on the west bank. We were in reserve, along with Creek Co, and were to join the attack and push through if the 325th faltered.

As the 325th's attack got underway the causeway became a mass of stagnant humanity. It became obvious more men were needed on the west bank to secure a viable bridgehead. At the time the 325th's attack was not moving forward, so General Gavin came over to me and said 'Rae, you've got to go and keep doing!'

We came out shouting, forcing our way through the log jam of dead and dying soldiers, and some soldiers refusing to continue the attack. We continued running until we reached the west bank. After we knocked out the German positions on the other side I split my force, sending half down a dirt road to the south, where the 325th was having trouble. I took the other half of my men and attacked west. We remained actively engaged until we made our way into Le Motey, spending the night there...." (Author's Note: For his action Robert Rae was awarded the DSC. He passed away in September 2003)

508th Parachute Infantry Regiment

The 3rd Battalion crossed over La Fiere Bridgehead at 1200 hours and attacked south to clear the area between Guetteville and the high ground. Contact was established with the 2nd Battalion, and the Merderet Bridgehead was thus extended to include both the causeways at La Fiere and southwest of Chef Du Pont. A sharp enemy counterattack from the direction of Amfreville was repulsed successfully between 1930 and 2100 hours. The remainder of the regiment maintained position, holding the Chef Du Pont Bridge. It received sporadic artillery fire during the evening.

82nd Airborne Division Artillery

The 456th Parachute Field Artillery Battalion and seaborne elements of the remainder of the Division Artillery units arrived. A group was made of the 456th Parachute and 320th Glider Field Artillery Battalions in direct support of the 325th GIR and 505th PIR. The 456th went into positions west of Neuville Au Plain with seven 75mm pack howitzers and fired its first rounds at 2130 hours. The 90th Division Artillery and one battalion of the 4th Division Artillery were in general support.

307th Airborne Engineer Battalion

The 1st Platoon, Company A, crossed the Merderet River with 1st Battalion, 325th GIR, north of La Fiere. The remainder of Company A supported the attack across La Fiere Bridge. The remainder of the Battalion salvaged equipment and resupply bundles, set up water points, and assembled one mile west of Sainte Mere Eglise.

Seaborne echelon

Force "C," under command of Brigadier General George P. Howell, closed into the Sainte Mere Eglise area.

Resupply

Two CG-4 gliders landed near Sainte Mere Eglise carrying greatly needed signal equipment. This constitued the second air resupply mission flown.

D plus 4, 10 June 1944

The Division was relieved along the bridgehead across the Merderet River by the 90th Infantry Division, which passed through the 82nd and continued the attack to the west. Despite the scattered parachute drops and isolation of some battalions, the Division secured the Meuville Au Plain - Sainte Mere Eglise - Chef Du Pont area within four days and established a firm bridgehead across the Merderet River from its junction with the Douve River to and including the railway bridge 1,500 yards north of La Fiere. Resistance had been stubborn and severe. Although it suffered heavy losses in the battle of the Merederet, the Division virtually destroyed the German 91st Infantry Division and prevented it from contacting the beach assault forces of the First U.S. Army. Although relieved in the merderet Bridgehead, Division troops continued the attack in the north.

325th Glider Infantry Regiment

The 357th infantry, 90th Division, passed through the 325th front line at 0540 hours. The 1st and 3rd Battalions remained in position throughout the day and night as a reserve.

505th Parachute Infantry Regiment

Supported by artillery, the 1st and 2nd Battalions jumped off across the canal at 1400 hours to seize Le Ham and Montebourg Station. The 1st Battalion by-passed Le Ham and seized the Station by 1800 hours in the face of stiff resistance throughout the advance. Elements of the 2nd Battalion were forced to withdraw from the outskirts of Le Ham at 2310 hours. Attempts to retake the town during the night were contested savagely. The 3rd Battalion remained in reserve, and the 2nd Battalion, 325th GIR attached, protected the regiment's southwestern flank.

507th Parachute Infantry Regiment

The 357th Infantry, 90th Division, passed through the 507th lines at 0540 hours. The Regiment assembled east of the Merderet River, in the vicinity of La Fiere, to reorganize and rest.

508th Parachute Infantry Regiment

The 358th Infantry, 90th Division, passed through the 508th lines at 0510 hours. The Regiment, less one company still at Le Port, assembled on high ground west of the Merderet River and reorganized.

Frank Staples, "D"Co, 508th PIR

During the evening of June 14, the 2nd Bn left "D"CO behind and moved into Coigny in a reserve position. Company D remained in defense north of Baupte with a combat group of six men, including Frank Staples, on the north end of the causeway, on the approach to the demolished railroad bridge southeast of the town. Another group guarded the demolished culvert west of the town.

At dawn on the 15th, according to the regimental history a force of enemy bicycle troops, estimated to be about fifty in number, attempted to cross the bridge west of Baupte. Two of the Germans surrended and nine were left dead in the road, while the rest retreated in disorder, abandoning most of their cycles:

"...A squad of Germans came down the road. Six of us opened fire at fifty feet. I can still see Joe Lizut, a Polack, throwing grenades over his head and laughing. We got every one of them. One of our boys was killed and one wounded. The fight lasted about two minutes...."

2nd Airborne Division Artillery

The 320th Glider and 456th Parachute Field Artillery Battalions, reinforced by the 915th Field Artillery Battalion, 90th Division, continued to fire harassing and interdiction missions in support of the 05th PIR.

Resupply

Two CG-4A gliders landed at Sainte Mere Eglise carrying signal quipment.

D plus 5 D plus 6, 11-12 June 1944

The Division secured the area north of Sainte Mere Eglise after ierce fighting. The 505th PIR, with 2nd Battalion, 325th GIR attached, seized Le Ham and drove the enemy north and northwest. With this action the 82nd Airborne Division delayed considerably the German 243rd Infantry Division from contracting the beach assault forces of the First U.S. Army.

325th Glider Infantry Regiment

After being passed through by the 359th Infantry, 90th DI, the regiment closed in an assembly area in the vicinity of Guetteville and rested and reorganized. The 2nd Battalion remained attached to the 505th.

> S.R. Hartline, 325th Glider Infantry Regiment
>
> "...We were ordered to attack at 0400. The Battalion's objective was Le Ham. The third Battalion had the main attack on the causeway. We were to their left to protect the left flank. We advanced up a hill to a hedgerow. There was a set of steps built to get over the hedgerow, and we were ordered to go over them. I was the fourth or fifth man to cross the steps. On the other side the hill sloped away, and we were exposed to the Germans in the next hedgerow. I had only gone ten to fifteen feet when a mortar shell hit on line between my comrade and me. I must have hit the ground before it landed. I got up and jumped the crater while the smoke was still rising.
>
> I made it to the end of the field, where there was an eight to ten foot drop. I didn't hesitate to jump. My comrade that was ahead of me said 'we moved to the next field,' and advanced only a short way when machine gun fire, mortar, and 88s came in on us in very concentrated fire. Our Company Commander, Captain Irvin Bloom, was killed, along with many of our comrades. I was pinned down. Finally a mortar shell hit the top of a tree I was laying under, and I was hit by shrapnel in my right leg and foot. I took the sulfa pills supplied for if hit and bandaged my wounds. We were under heavy barrage for three hours or more. When it finally eased up I tried to make my way to the rear. I crawled behind the hedgerow until I came to a French farmhouse.
>
> They motioned me to go into the house, and I didn't know whether any Germans were in there or not. They assured me there weren't any. They were a very old couple. He was minus a leg from WWI, and a brother had had his hand amputated, probably from WWI. The lady fixed me an egg with bread and gave me a glass of wine. I then was given a shot glass with a clear liquid in it which I drank, but had a hard time getting my breath. This was my first introduction to Calvados.
>
> After dark, two soldiers from the 505th PIR helped me back to the field aid station. When I woke up the next morning and looked around most of the troops there were from my company.
>
> At dusk on 10 June we were loaded on six-by-six trucks. There were nine stretchers loaded on the seat level, and nine across the side boards on top. We had just arrived at the landing craft they were to load us on to be taken to the hospital ship when all the aids hit the ground. A German plane flew at low altitude along the line of landing craft being loaded. No one was hit. The medics had given the pilot the name "Bedcheck Charlie," because the plane made the pass at the same time every night.
>
> The next morning, when we awoke, we found the LST we were on was sitting on the sand, waiting for the tide to come in. It was an hour or so before we were afloat, and they took us out to a Hospital Ship, on which we were put aboard. We landed at Southampton and were taken by train to the 55th General Hospital, Malvern on the Green, Wells."

505th Parachute Infantry Regiment

The 2nd Battalion, with the 2nd Battalion, 325th GIR attached, on the left, attacked at 1130 hours to capture Le Ham. Overcoming severe opposition in wet and difficult terrain, the 2nd Battalion, 325th, seized Le Ham at 2025 hours. By 2300 hours positions were consolidated along the entire Merderet River, up to and including the Montebourg railroad station. Contact with the 8th Infantry, 4th Infantry Division, was made by the 1st Battalion at Montebourg station. The bridge over the Merderet River was blown by U.S. troops at 2145. The Regiment remained in position, patrolling west across the river until relieved by the 357th Infantry, 90th Division, during the night of 12-13 June.

507th Parachute Infantry Regiment

The Regiment continued to rest and reorganize in the vicinity of La Fiere

Captain David Brummit, S-3, 507th PIR

"...On the ground I was unable to locate any identifiable, and after daylight discovered from a French farmer that we were near the village of Graignes, which was not to be found on my tactical map. Fortunately I had been issued an escape kit that included a silk map of Normandy, which I examined, and to my dismay discovered we had been dropped approximately 18 km from our assigned drop zone near Amfreville. To this day I have not received a credible explanation of the Troop Carrier actions, but the resulting mistake proved to be very costly to the 507th, and to the 3rd Battalion mission in particular. As assembly continued into D-Day troopers, including Major Johnson, gravitating to Graignes finally totaled 173 officers and men from the 507th, plus 7 troopers from the 101st Airborne Division and one glider pilot. Later we added two Spanish civilians who had been forced into a German labor unit, both of whom spoke French, thereby supplementing our one French speaking 3rd Battalion soldier. Major Johnson assumed command and established an abbreviated CP in the local schoolhouse. Our mission required us to join our parent unit with the greatest possible speed. Otherwise the ability of the 3rd Bn to accomplish its mission would be drastically reduced to small unit actions. With this thought uppermost in mind, I made a reconnaissance and observed what appeared to be a portion of the 101st Division attacking German forces in Carentan, approximately 8 km distant, on line between us and the 82nd Division area, which of course included the 507th. Up to this time we had had no German contact in our vicinity, and there did not appear to be any major German activity between the 101st Division and us.

In my capacity as Battalion S-3, I formulated a tentative night-march plan to go through the flooded swamp area that we had waded, finding it to be waist to chest deep, or alternatively to go around the surrounding coastline to Carentan, link up with the U.S. force there, and continue on to the 82nd Division area. The plan had its negative aspects: 81mm mortars would have to be spiked, ammunition destroyed, and various other equipment abandoned. Additionallly, the swamp appeared to include canals of unknown depths, requiring us to swim a short distance or requisition two or three of the small fishing boats observed nearby for ferry use in accommodating the heavy equipment and non-swimmers. I considered our Battalion Mission to be critical, overriding these obstacles and worthy of our best effort. I presented the plan to Major Johnson, who rejected it curtly, turning aside my forceful reference to our stated Mission. Instead, Major Johnson directed that we remain in place, organize a perimeter defense around the village of Graignes, and await a link-up with ground forces coming across the beach. That decision entailed an on-the-spot reorganization of our specialist personnel into provisional infantry fire teams reinforced by the machine gun and mortar platoons. During the ensuing days the officers and men proved beyond a doubt that they were elite troops of the highest order. They went on both reconnaissance and combat patrols, mined the key Graignes bridge, manned outpost and perimeter defense positions set up with protective fire, targeted gaps with pre-planned mortar fire, and established wire and radio communications throughout the position. The Command Post and the Battalion Aid Station became operational. The position was improved as sporadic contact was made with German forces. On D+4 a German scout was killed. His papers identified him as a member of the reconnaissance battalion of an Armored Division.

On Sunday, June 11th, the Germans launched a massive attack with a large infantry force variously estimated at plus or minus a regiment and reinforced with artillery. Judging by the black uniforms found later on dead German soldiers, the attacking force contained SS troops. The attack increased in intensity throughout the afternoon and night hours. Wire communications were cut, and radio communications became undependable. I took part in several firefights while visiting defensive positions. As the last position was being outflanked, I ordered the crew members of the remaining light machine gun to withdraw to a previously designated fall back position. During the movement both crewmembers were killed. I discarded my carbine, scooped up the machine gun (minus the damaged tripod) and the box of ammunition, and leaped over a stone wall from which two troopers were giving me covering fire. As I reached their side both were killed by small arms fire. I heard no more from that sector. There was a lull in the fighting, and not having received any recent communication from Major Johnson, I moved to another firing position behind a stone wall near the church. Battalion Sergeant Major Salewski approached me with information that Major gave the order to abandon the position and attempt to return individually to friendly lines. He and others in the command post had gone. I walked over to the CP and found the report to be accurate. I did discover, however, that the Battalion S-1 (Lt. Wagner), plus a number of other troopers, were still in firing positions nearby. Also, our two French speaking Spanish civilians were still with us. Later, it was reported that Major Johnson had been killed during the move. The battlefield was silent as I pondered this information, and automatically I began an estimate of the situation. Darkness had fallen some time before, and the German attack had ceased, perhaps for the night. However, they most likely would resume at daylight. Our chances of survival would be slim indeed if we continued to defend the position. A night withdrawal to my earlier-recommended march-plan assembly area, for those of us remaining, appeared to offer a chance to reach the 507th area. From the assembly area we could move into the swamps, and thereafter implement my march-plan toward the 101st Division.

I was unaware of it until the following day, but the Battalion Surgeon, his medics, and a number of wounded troopers in the Aid Station some distance away from the CP area had not departed. Had I been aware of this situation I would have made a specific move to bring them along. I do not know whether the Surgeon did not receive Johnson's order, or whether he and his people chose to remain, expecting to be treated as prisoners of war by the Germans. I learned much later that all of that group had been murdered by the enemy..."

508th Parachute Infantry Regiment

The Regiment continued to rest and reorganize in the vicinity of the high ground west of the Merderet River. Contact was maintained with the 101st Airborne Division on the left. Preparations were completed on 12 June for an attack to establish a bridgehead over the Douve River, at Beuzeville La Bastille, on the night of 12-13 June.

O.B.Hill. Hq Co, 1st Bn, 508th PIR

"...Along the way we picked up more jumpers, and soon discovered that we were not the only ones who were not in the proper place. We found men from the 505th, some from the 507th, and even some from the 101st Division. The 101st was scheduled to land around Carentan, which was several miles from our area. At just before daybreak we encountered a group of German soldiers at a crossroad, and we engaged in a fierce fire fight that lasted about 20 minutes. The time is a pure guess, but it seemed much longer. We drove them off and continued moving in the chosen direction.

We were challenged two other times before we reached one of the main roads. At each of these points we drove the enemy off. We were outnumbered each time, and the only explanation for our coming out ahead is that we were more determined and perhaps better trained. We lost some of our men also. That was our first experience, and it is not a good one. We had been trained for this, and we had been told what to expect, but seeing it first hand was not a good experience.

At about 1000 AM this first morning we had arrived at the village of Beuzeville. This is on the east side of the Douve River, across from the town of Beuzeville La Bastille. We were at the bridge that our unit was supposed to destroy, but we did not know that at the time. We were still under the impression that we had landed on the east side of the Merderet River. We had no idea where we were until later in the day.

There was a pocket of German soldiers at this crossroad, and we discovered that there were more of our group across the road from us. Together we drove the Germans off, and we crossed the road to join the others. We then thought that there were still more of our men across the road where we had been. They were, we thought, just up the road, and Mel Beets from my company volunteered to go get them and guide them to where we were. It turned out that the men up the road were the enemy, and Mel was captured.

The two groups now assembled in fields behind a row of about seven houses along the road in Beuzeville. I located S/Sgt Ray Hummel from my company. We then realized that he and I were the ranking men in our group. We had no officers. We compared notes and determined that we were in Beuzeville. We could see where the two rivers came together beyond where we were. In fact, we were surrounded on two sides by flood waters from the two rivers. In order to try and determine which way we should go or what we should do, Ray and I thought we should get up in one the two story houses and see what was around us.

We shot the lock off the back door of the fourth house from the river. The house was occupied, and the people in it were badly scared. They did not interfere; in fact, they smiled at us and gave us the run of the place. Ray and I went up the stairs just inside the back door, and we were followed by Jim McMahon, who was then the corporal in the wire section of my company. Ray and I went to a double window on the front of the house and were looking to see what was around us. We heard tanks approaching from the west, and we dropped down to keep from being seen. It was three French Renault tanks that the German Army were using in that area. The center one stopped immediately under the window where we were. The top hatch opened, and one of the soldiers inside stood up to look around. While he was looking I handed Hummel a Gammon grenade, and he dropped it into the tank. That tank was knocked out of action, and the other two were trying to figure what had hit it.

We left that building and once again joined the men in the fields behind the houses. If the two tanks had pursued us we could not have stopped them, because the heaviest weapon we had was our rifles...." (Author's Note: OB. Hill was Chairman of the 508th PIR Association after the war; he passed away in 2002.)

82nd Airborne Division Artillery
The 456th Parachute Field Arttillery Battalion remained in direct support of the 505th. The 320th Glider Field Artillery Battalion prepared to reinforce the fire of the 319th Glider Field Artillery Battalion and moved south of Picauville. The 319th, in direct support of the 508th, moved west across the Douve River into positions north of Beuzeville la Bastille. The 915th Field Artillery Battalion, attached from the 90th Infantry Division, was relieved. The 188th Field Artillery Battalion (105mm howitzer) was attached and moved into positions to reinforce the fire of the 319th.

307th Airborne Engineer Battalion
The Battalion continued to salvage resupply bundles and operate water points in the area. Extensive surveys of the Douve River were conducted during this period, and bridging material, assault boats, and other river crossing equipment were obtained.

Attached units
Company C, 746th Tank Battalion, was relieved from attachment to the Division.

D plus 7, 13 June 1944

The Division, using the 508th PIR, extended its right flank by establishing a bridgehead across the Douve River, at Beuzeville La Bastille, and contacted the 101st Airborne Division again at Baupte. Other elements of the Division continued to reorganize and regroup in preparation to moving through the 90th Infantry Division and attacking to the west in conjunction with the 9th Infantry Division. The Division Command Post moved to a point near Picauville.

325th Glider Infantry Regiment
The 2nd Battalion rejoined the regiment at 1000 hours. The regiment closed in a new assembly area south of Picauville at 1630 hours. Preparations were made to attack to the west the following day.

505th Parachute Infantry Regiment
The 2nd Battalion, 325th GIR, was relieved from attachment. The regiment moved from the Le Ham area to an assembly area east of Picauville and rested and reorganized.

507th Parachute Infantry Regiment
The regiment moved from the La Fiere area to an assembly area north of Picauville. Preparations were made to attack to the west the following day.

508th Parachute Infantry Regiment
A combat team composed of the regiment, the 319th Glider Field Artillery Battalion, Battery A, 80th Airborne Antiaircraft Battalion, a detachment from the 307th Airborne Engineer Battalion, and one platoon of Troop B, 4th Cavalry Reconnaissance Squadron, attacked south across the Douve River. Company F crossed the Douve by assault boats at 0001 hours and seized Beuzeville La bastille. The remainder of the troops crossed the river on a footbridge constructed by engineers, beginning at 0400 hours. The 1st Battalion cleared Cretteville by 0745 hours, destroyed considerable enemy equipment, including 12 light tanks, and occupied defensive positions at Coigny. The 2nd Battalion met determined resistance outside of Baupte, but occupied the town by 1800 and established contact with the 101st Airborne Division to the south. The 3rd Battalion secured the area between Pont Auny and Hotot. During the entire action 14 light tanks were knocked out, and sizable quantities of enemy equipment were captured or destroyed.

82nd Airborne division Artillery
The 319th and 320th Glider and 188th Field Artillery Battalions fired in support of the 508th PIR's crossing of the Douve River at Beuzeville La Bastille. These three battalions expended 1,880 rounds in 50 minutes, and their fire was reinforced by the 90th Division Artillery. The 319th displaced south of the Douve River at 1800 hours. The 456th Parachute Field Artillery Battalion moved from the Le Ham sector into positions north of Picauville at 1800 hours.

80th Airborne Antiaircraft Battalion

Battery A knocked out fire from enemy light tanks in conjunction with the 1st Battalion, 508th PIR's attack south of the Douve River

307th Airborne Engineer Battalion

Company A operated assault boats across the Douve River at Beuzeville La Bastille beginning at 0001 hours in support of the 508th. A footbridge was constructed first and, with the assistance of VII Corps Engineers, a Bailey bridge was completed by 0830 hours. The 3rd Platoon of Company B was attached to the 508th and prepared the bridge south of Baupte for demolition.

Attached Troops

Company A, 746th Tank Battalion, was attached to the Division at 1700 hours.

Resupply

Eleven gliders carrying ordnance and signal equipment landed at Sainte Mere Eglise.

D plus 8, 14 June 1944

The Division continued to mop up in the Baupte area, and also passed through the 90th Division to attack west toward Saint Sauveur Le vicomte.

The Attack, with the 82nd Airborne Division on the left and the 9th Infantry Division on the right, originally was scheduled to begin shortly after dawn, but was delayed until 1000 to permit units being relieved additional opportunity to seize the contemplated line of departure. The attack began at 1000 even though the line of departure had not been seized. The fighting was a bitter, hedgerow-to-hedgerow onslaught, but considerable progress was made.

325th Glider Infantry Regiment

The regiment attacked at 1000 in columns of battalions, with the 3rd Battalion leading. The 507th PIR was to the regiment's right. As the scheduled line of departure had not been seized, the 325th attacked to the right of the 358th Infantry, 90th Division, instead of through it, but later swung in front of that regiment. The main highway due west of Etienville was strongly defended by the enemy, but they were driven off the road by 1830 hours after exceptionally hard fighting and repeated thrusts by both the 3rd and 1st Battalions, supported by one platoon of Company A, 746th Tank Battalion. The 1st Battalion continued to attack and advanced west 400 yards. The regiment consolidated its positions at 2100 hours, established firm contact with the 507th on the right, and prepared to continue the attack to the west.

505th Parachute Infantry Regiment

The regiment remained in Division reserve. Company I moved to secure the bridge south of Etienville (Pont l'AbbÈ), holding positions at the north end of the bridge. Company H was attached to the 325th GIR at 1400 hours to act as Infantry escort for a platoon of Company A, 746th Tank Battalion, through and beyond Etienville, but the company reverted to regimental control at 1940 hours. The regiment was ordered at 2100 hours to move into position 1,000 yards north of Etienville. Company F remained at the Etienville Bridge and established patrol contact with the 508th in the Beuzeville La Bastille Bridgehead.

507th Parachute Infantry Regiment

Attacking in columns of battalions with 3rd Battalion leading, the regiment crossed the creek between Renouf and Etienville at 1000 hours, passing through the 90th Division. The 325th GIR was on the left, and the 60th Infantry, 9th Division, was on the right. Encountering heavy pounding by enemy artillery, the 3rd Battalion turned north to block Renouf and protect the north flank of the Division, while the 9th Division spent the better part of the day seizing the town. Enemy resistance was severe. Counterattacks in the evening were repulsed with the assistance of one platoon of tanks from Company A, 746th Tank Battalion. The 2nd and 1st Battalions in that order followed the 3rd Battalion and continued the attack to the west, reaching the outskirts of La Bonneville by 2200 hours. After consoldating positions and reorganizing, all Battalions prepared to continue the attack the next day.

508th Parachute Infantry Regiment

The 1st Battalion moved from the vicinity of Coigny to assist the 2nd Battalion clear Baupte at 0130 hours. The 3rd Battalion repelled a sharp counterattack at 0700 hours in the vicinity of Hotot. The ennemy attempted to break through the 3rd Battalion positions again at 1005 hours, but the attack failed after the enemy sustained heavy casualties. The highway and railroad bridges southwest of Hotot were blown by attached elements of the 307th Airborne Engineer Battalion; they moved from Baupte to the northwest at 1030 and attacked Pont Auny to dislodge an enemy concentration building up in that area. After a sharp fire fight the 1st Battalion broke contact at 1600 hours and withdrew toward Baupte, assembling in a reserve position in the vicinity of Francquetot. The 2nd Battalion left Company D at Baupte and moved at 2300 hours to a position in the vicinity of Coigny.

82nd Airborne Division Artillery

The 319th Glider Field Artillery Battalion remained in direct support of the 508th and fired 600 rounds against enemy buildups in the

Hotot area. The 320th Glider and 456th Parachute Field Artillery Battalions were placed in direct support of the attacking 325th GIR and 507th, respectively. The 188th field Artillery Battalion was in direct support. More than 2,200 rounds were fired in support of the attack toward the west. The 80th Armored Field Artillery Battalion was attached to the Division at 0900 hours and moved into position north of Etienville.

80th Airborne Antiaircraft Battalion
Batteries A and B remained attached to the 508th. Battery C was attached to the 507th. The remainder of the Battalion remained in reserve.

307th Airborne Engineer Battalion
One platoon of Company B was attached to the 508th and blew the culvert and the railroad bridge southwest of Hotot at 1800 hours. The bridge at Cretteville was blown by the 508th. The platoon reverted to Company control at 2300 hours. Company A continued to provide security for bridges at Beuzeville la Bastille and performed reconnaissance work along the 508th PIR and 325th GIR fronts.

Attached Troops
Company A, 746th Tank Battalion, supported the Division's attack to the west, with one platoon each attached to the 325th and 507th regiments. Tanks were withdrawn at nightfall into an assembly area north of Picauville.

Resupply
Four 75mm pack howitzers were flown by C-47 to Sainte Mere Eglise.

D plus 9, 15 June 1944

The Division continued the hedgerow-to-hedgerow attack, but shortly after nightfall it became apparent that the crust of the enemy resistance west of the Douve River had been broken. The 505th PIR relieved the 507th PIR after a strong enemy counterattack in the flank, supported by tanks, halted the 507th advance. The Division Command Post moved west of Etienville.

325th Glider Infantry Regiment
The Regiment attacked (in the order 1st, 2nd, and 3rd Battalions) at 0500 hours, and reached the creek southwest of La Bonneville by 0810 hours, meeting only moderate resistance. Tanks from Company A, 746th Tank Battalion, supported the attack.

505th Parachute Infantry Regiment
The regiment attacked to the west, passing through the 507th in the latter's zone at 1500. Battery C, 80th Airborne Antiaircraft Battalion, and one platoon of Company A, 746th Tank Battalion, were attached. Moderately strong enemy opposition was encountered, and by nightfall the regiment had advanced to the creek line north of Crosville. Company I, guarding the bridge at Etienville, was relieved by the 507th and reverted to regimental control.

507th Parachute Infantry Regiment
The regiment attacked at 0500 hours and advanced 600 yards, meeting little opposition up to 0630 hours. One platoon of Company A, 746th Tank Battalion, moved up to forward positions at 0615 to support the regiment. A heavy counterattack the right flank, launched by the enemy at 0930 hours and supported by tanks, halted the advance of the regiment. However, the 507th, recovering from the heavy artillery and mortar fire, ejected the enemy force that had penetrated its lines and reestablished its front by 1500 hours, at which time the 505th passed through the 507th. The regiment then assembled, moved to Etienville, and later crossed the Douve River into the Cretteville-Baupte area preparatory to relieving the 508th. Company B relieved Company I, 505th, at the bridge at Etienville.

508th Parachute Infantery Regiment
The regiment continued active defense of the Cretteville-Baupte sector, repulsing enemy attempts to break through in the vicinity of Hotot and Baupte. The 2nd Battalion relieved the 3rd Battalion near Pont Auny. The 3rd Battalion assembled and moved north of the Douve River into Division reserve one-half mile west of La Bonneville. The remainder of the regiment prepared to join the 3rd Battalion upon completion of relief by the 507th during the night of 15-16 June.

82nd Airborne Division Artillery
The 319th Glider Field Artillery Battalion remained in position and prepared to support the 507th moving into Beuzeville La Bastille Bridgehead. The 456th Parachute Field Artillery Battalion changed to support the 505th when the latter relieved the 507th, and with the 320th Glider Field Artillery Battalion displaced to positions north and west of Etienville. Division Artillery, with the 188th Field Artillery Battalion (155mm Howitzers), in general support of the Division's attack to the west, fired more than 4,800 rounds in all types of missions. Company B, 87th Chemical Mortar Battalion (4,2 inch mortars), was attached in the vicinity of Etienville at 1130 hours.

80th Airborne Antiaircraft Battalion
Battery A was relieved from attachment to the 508th. Batteries B and C were attached to the 507th and 508th, respectively.

Attached Troops

In the attack to the west the following troops were attached to the Division and assisted materially in the accomplisment of the mission:

- Company A, 746th Tank Battalion. (One platoon was attached to the 325th GIR, and one was attached first to the 507th and later to the 505th).
- Troop B, 4th Cavalry Reconnaissance Squadron
- 87th Armored Field Artillery Battalion
- 188th Field Artillery Battalion
- Company C, 899th Tank Destroyer Battalion (in Division reserve)
- Company B, 87th Chemical Mortar Battalion (attached to Division Artillery)

D plus 10, 16 June 1944

The Division, attacking to the west and protecting the southern flank of VII Corps during the Corps' operation to seize Cherbourg, forged ahead against the German 77th Infantry Division. The Division routed the enemy in its sector, drove across the Douve River, and established a firm bridgehead around Saint Sauveur Le Vicomte.

The orders from Corps were to "seize the line of the Douve and prepare to continue the attack to the west," however, upon arriving on the east bank of the Douve it was quite obvious that the German forces were in a state of complete confusion. The Division Commander immediately requested Corps for authority to cross, but because of difficulties in communication an immediate answer was not obtained. Seizing the initiative after personal reconnaissance, General Ridgway ordered the 2nd Battalion, 505th to cross without delay. By the time clearance had been obtained from Corps two battalions had crossed the river and established a secure bridgehead for further operations.

In three days of fierce hedgerow-to-hedgerow fighting the Division pushed the enemy steadily westwards, and made it possible for the 9th Infantry Division to drive to the sea and cut the Cherbourh Peninsula in two. A forward Division Command Post was established in a chateau just east of Saint Sauveur Le Vicomte and the Douve River. A new force "A" was formed to include the 505th and 508th and established its headquarters in Saint Sauveur Le Vicomte.

325th Glider Infantry Regiment

The 325th continued the attack and reached its assigned objectives on the east bank of the Douve River, overlooking Saint Sauveur Le Vicomte, at 0930 hours. The regiment consolidated positions and patrolled aggressively across the Douve River.

505th Parachute Infantry Regiment

The regiment continued to the west and reached its objectives on high ground east of the Douve River, overlooking Saint Sauveur Le Vicomte, by 1130 hours. Finding the enemy in a high state of confusion, the 2nd Battalion crossed the river and seized Saint Sauveur Le Vicomte. The 1st Battalion followed and pressed on to secure an area 2,000 yards in depth. The 3rd Battalion was relieved by the 3rd Bn, 508th, at 1540 of its mission to protect the right flank of the Division. This Battalion then crossed the river and attacked to the north at Saint Sauveur Le Vicomte to seize and hold the crossroads. By 2230 the bridgehead was secure and approximately 2,000 to 3,000 yards in depth.

507th Parachute Infantry Regiment

The regiment completed relief of the 508th at 0415 in the Cretteville-Baupte area. The 2nd Battalion took up positions between Baupte and Coigny, and the 3rd Battalion defended a line from Coigny to Francquetot. The 1st Battalion was in reserve in Francquetot. The entire area was subjected to heavy enemy artillery and mortar fire.

508th Parachute Infantry Regiment

After relief by the 507th, the regiment closed into reserve positions northwest of Etienville at 0900 hours. The 3rd Battalion relieved the 3rd Bn, 505th, in the vicinity of Crosville, with the mission of protecting the Division's north flank. The 1st and 2nd Battalions moved into position north of Rauville, and at 2200 hours moved into the Saint Sauveur Le Vicomte - La Haye Du Puits Highway.

82nd Airborne Division Artillery

Until troops crossed the Douve River, fire was massed on routed enemy columns and convoys in and around Saint Sauveur Le Vicomte. All battalions, except the 319th Glider Field Artillery Battalion in the Cretteville-Baupte sector, displaced forward. At 1830 hours the 172nd Field Artillery Battalion (4,5 inch guns) was attached and went into positions immediately to the east of Saint Sauveur Le Vicomte. Artillery liaison planes arrived from a base in England.

80th Airborne Antiaircraft Battalion

Battery A remained in reserve. Battery B was attached to the 507th, and Battery C supported the attack of the 505th. The remainder of the Battalion was in reserve.

307th Airborne Engineer Battalion

The Battalion continued extensive reconnaissance of the Douve River and supported the attack against Saint Sauveur Le Vicomte.

Attached Troops

Company A, 746th Tank Battalion, supported the attack of the Division, attaching one platoon to each of the two assault regiments. Tanks crossed the Douve River into the Saint Sauveur Le Vicomte Bridgehead. One platoon from Company C, 899th Tank Destroyer Battalion, was attached to the 3rd Battalion, 508th, and another to the 505th. Company B, 87th Chemical Mortar Battalion, was relieved from support of the 325th GIR and was placed in support of the 505th. It remained, however, attached to Division Artillery.

D Plus 11 and 12, 17-18 June 1944

During this period the Division secured the Bridgehead at Saint Sauveur Le Vicomte, reorganized, and prepared to attack south of Etienville to extend its southern boundary. The 9th Infantry Division passed through the bridgehead and attacked to the west coast of the peninsula.

325th Glider Infantry Regiment

The regiment moved to an assembly area southeast of Etienville on 17 June and made plans to cross the Douve River south of Etienville.

505th Parachute Infantry Regiment

The 505th cleared the Saint Sauveur Le Vicomte Bridgehead to a depth of 3,000 yards of all enemy pockets of resistance, consolidated defensive positions north and west of Saint Sauveur Le Vicomte, and effected passage of the 47th Infantry, 9th Infantry Division, through its lines to continue the attack to the west. The regiment patrolled extensively, and rested and reorganized.

507th Parachute Infantry Regiment

The regiment continued to hold defensive positions in the Cretteville-Baupte area and patrolled extensively, concentrating its efforts along the western front. Contact was maintained with adjacent units.

508th Parachute Infantry Regiment

The 1st and 2nd Battalions cleared the bridgehead of all enemy resistance south and west of Saint Sauveur Le Vicomte. Company C established a roadblock and blew the bridge on the Saint Sauveur Le Vicomte-La Haye Du Puits across the Prairies Marecageuses. Company A reinforced Company C on 18 June. The 3rd Battalion remained in position, protecting the north flank of the Division until 18 June, when it moved to the bank of the Douve River, west of Etienville.

82nd Airborne Division Artillerie

The 456th Parachute Field Artillery Battalion, reinforced by the 172n Field Artillery Battalion, continued to support the 505th and 508th ir the Saint Sauveur Le Vicomte Bridgehead. The remainder of Divi sion Artillery—less the 319th Glider Field Artillery Battalion, whicl supported the 507th in the Cretteville-Baupte area—moved bacl into positions north of Etienville and made preparations to suppor the attack south of Etienville, across the Douve River.

80th Airborne Antiaircraft Battalion

Battery A was attached to the 2nd Battalion, 508th, and Battery D (5(caliber MG) moved into position, protecting the bridge at Sain Sauveur Le Vicomte. Battery E made preparations to support th attack of the Division south of Etienville, across the Douve River

307th Airborne Engineer Battalion

Company A procured river crossing materiel and prepared to assis the crossing of the Douve River, south of Etienville. The Battalior continued to reconnoiter the Douve River.

Attached Troops

Tanks of Company A, 746th Tank Battalion, and armored cars o Company C, 899th Tank Destroyer Battalion, moved into reserve positions and prepared to revert to parent units. Troop B, 4th Cavalry Reconnaissance Squadron, patrolled extensively to the wes and north and south, reporting valuable information on enemy movements and dispositions.

Resupply

The last air resupply mission was flown on 18 June, when 5,00(Gammon grenades were landed by C-47 at Sainte Mere Eglise.

D plus 13, 19 June 1944

The Division crossed the Douve River south of Etienville, and established a fire bridgehead extending south to Pretot. Contact was made with the troops in the Cretteville-Baupte area, and the entire Division area south of the Douve was cleared of the enemy. The 90th Infantry Division relieved the 82nd of the responsability of guarding Saint Sauveur le Vicomte. The Division was attached to VII Corps, which had the mission of protecting the south flank of VI Corps in the VII Corps' assault to the north of Cherbourg.

325th Glider Infantry Regiment

The 2nd Battalion crossed the Douve River southeast of Etienville and west of Montessy by assault boats at 2350 hours the night o

18-19 June. The crossing was accomplished without incident. A feint by one squad distracted the enemy's attention to the area west of Etienville. Supported by an artillery barrage the 1st Battalion, followed by the 3rd Bn, crossed over an engineer footbridge beginning at 0215 hours and attacked against slight opposition to the south to join forces with the 2nd Battalion, which was attacking the enemy force defending the bridgehead area from the rear. By 0730 hours the 2nd Battalion had been passed through by the 1st and 3rd Battalions, and the regiment held an area extending from Le Hau de Haut along the edge of the Bois de Limors, thence north of La Danguerie to Vindefontaine. The 3rd Battalion, 508th (Lt. Colonel Louis Mendez) was attached to the 325th and crossed at the same point as the 2nd Battalion. It attacked on the regiment's left flank to pass through the 1st Battalion, 507th, in Vindefontaine, and to seize Pretot. Enemy resistance increased, but the regiment finally broke through and extended its lines securely to a depth of 3,000 yards south of the Douve River by 2000 hours. The engineers completed a bridge south of Etienville by 1730, thus permitting supporting artillery and vehicles to join the regiment.

505th Parachute Infantry Regiment

Late in the evening the regiment moved by truck from the Saint Sauveur Le Vicomte area to an assembly area south of Les Moitiers en Bauptois in the bridgehead established during the day by the 325th GIR.

507th Parachute Infantry Regiment

The 1st Battalion attacked across the bridge west of Cretteville at 0015 hours to seize Vindefontaine in conjunction with the attack by the 325th to establish a bridgehead south of Etienville. After bitter fighting and considerable sniping the Battalion reached its objective by 0740 hours, and spent the remainder of the day clearing the town of snipers and pockets of enemy resistance. At 1405 hours the 3rd Battalion, 508th, passed through the 3rd Battalion lines. The remainder of the 507th stayed in position in the Cretteville-Baupte sector.

508th Parachute Infantry Regiment

The regiment was relieved of the responsability of guarding the Saint Sauveur le Vicomte area at 1440 and assembled prior to moving to join the remainder of the Division. The 3rd Battalion, attached to the 325th, crossed the Douve River in assault boats southeast of Etienville and west of Montessy at 0700 hours. The crossing was made without incident, and the battalion proceeded south, meeting increasing resistance. At 1405 hours this battalion passed through the 507th positions at Vindefontaine and pushed on to the outskirts of Pretot. Here an enemy strongpoint held up the advance temporarily.

82nd Airborne Division Artillery

The 320th Glider, 87th Armored, and 188th Field Artillery Battalions supported the attack of the 325th GIR and crossed the river into the bridgehead area during the late afternoon and night. The 172nd Field Artillery Battalion was relieved from attachment to the Division. The 319th Glider Field Artillery Battalion moved into the bridgehead area and wes placed in direct support of the 325th. The 320th Glider Field Artillery Battalion was placed in direct support of the 505th.

80th Airborne Antiaircraft Battalion

Battery B supported the attack of the 1st Battalion, 507th. Two 57mm guns were ferried across the river with the 2nd Battalion, 325th GIR. At least three enemy light tanks were knocked out in the action in the bridgehead. Battery C crossed into the bridgehead late in the afternoon. Batteries D and E went into position to provide antiaircraft protection to the Etienville Bridge.

307th Airborne Engineer Battalion

Company A used 25 assault boats to ferry attacking troops across the Douve River, southeast of Etienville and west of Montessy. Company B erected footbridges at Etienville and Vindefontaine for the infantry, and later, under enemy shellfire, erected a vehicular bridge at Vindefontaine by 0400 hours and a class 40 bridge by 2100 hours. Assistance was given to Corps engineers in repairing the bridge and causeway south of Etienville.

Attached Troops

Company C, 899th Tank Destroyer Battalion, was relieved from attachment to the Division at 1400 hours, and Company A, 607th Tank Destroyer Battalion, was attached at 1800 hours. Company B, 87th Chemical Mortar Battalion, supported the 325th GIR from positions in the vicinity of the 2nd Battalion crossing. Company A, 746th Tank Battalion, was attached to the 325th. Troop B, 4th Cavalry Reconnaissance Squadron, continued patrolling activities. The 87th Armored and 188th Field Artillery Battalions remained attached to the Division, but the 172nd Field Artillery Battalion was relieved at 1100 hours.

D plus 14, 20 June 1944

The Division Command Post moved south of Etienville and south of the Douve River.

325th Glider Infantry Regiment

The regiment consolidated positions, strengthened the defenses of the bridgehead, and patrolled into enemy lines.

505th Parachute Infantry Regiment

The 3rd Battalion moved into the Bois De Limors and occupied positions along the western edge after encountering only slight enemy opposition initially. Later it came under intense mortar and artillery fire. The rest of the regiment remained in an assembly area south of Les Moitiers en Bauptois, having crossed into the area at 0150 hours.

507th Parachute Infantry Regiment

The 1st Battalion remained in position around Vindefontaine until 2330 hours, when it relieved the 3rd Battalion. Other elements of the regiment remained in the Cretteville-Baupte sector, preparing to be relieved by the 90th Infantry Division.

508th Parachute Infantry Regiment

The regiment was passed through by the 90th Infantry Division troops west of Saint Sauveur Le Vicomte and moved south of the Douve River, closing into an assembly area southwest of Les Moitiers en Bauptois by 1330 hours. The 3rd Battalion launched a determined attack against Pretot at 0600 hours, seized the town, and took up defensive positions after a sharp, short battle. The Battalion was subjected to heavy artillery and mortar shelling throughout the day. At 1600 hours the Battalion moved to positions west of Pretot and was relieved in place at 2330 hours by the 1st Battalion, 507th PIR.

D plus 15 to D plus 24, 21-30 June 1944

During this period, which was marked by sharp local actions, the Division secured and held its area with a front generally that of D plus 14. An VIII Corps attack had been planned for late on 22 June, in which the Division was to seize the high ground overlooking La Haye Du Puits, while the 90th Infantry Division, thrusting from both flanks, would pinch the Division out and seize the town. This attack was postponed until 3 July because of a very severe storm in the English Channel that interrupted lines of communication and supply, and necessitated restriction of ammunition and ordnance lines. The first U.S. Army placed priority on its attack to seize the vital port of Cherbourg, which fell to VII Corps on 26 June. Meanwhile the Division reorganized, regrouped, and patrolled aggressively and extensively. On 26 June the Division participated in a simulated Corps attack, firing all possible weapons between 0730 and 0800.

325th Glider Infantry Regiment

The 2nd Battalion was relieved on 24 June by 3rd Battalion, 508th, and the regiment then held a line between the 508th on the right and the 507th on the left. The 1st Battalion was on the right of the regimental sector, 2nd Battalion on the left, and 3rd Battalion in reserve. During the entire period the regiment remained in position, patrolled extensively, and made preparations for attack to the west.

505th Parachute Infantry Regiment

The 3rd Battalion remained in position in the western sector of the Bois De Limors until relieved by the 1st Battalion on 22 June. The 2nd Battalion took over defense of the eastern sector at the same time. On 26 June the 3rd Battalion relieved 2nd Battalion and, in turn, the 3rd Battalion was relieved by the 1st Battalion, 508th PIR attached, on 29 June. During the entire period it occupied the bois de Limors the regiment suffered losses from heavy enemy mortar and artillery concentrations. Extensive patrolling was carried out, contact with adjacent units was established firmly, and firing was held to a minimum so that friendly positions would not be disclosed.

507th Parachute Infantry Regiment

The 1st Battalion remained in position on the high ground west of Pretot. The 2nd and 3rd Battalions in the Cretteville-Baupte sector were relieved by the 359th Infantry, 90th Infantry Division, and moved into reserve positions, backing up the 1st Battalion to the north of Pretot. The 2nd Battalion relieved the 3rd Battalion, 508th, in the latter's sector on 30 June and became attached to the 508th. During the entire period the regiment patrolled aggressively into enemy lines.

508th Parachute Infantry Regiment

The 1st Battalion occupied defensive positions northeast of Vindefontaine on 22 June and remained there until relieved by the 507th on 24 June. On the same day the 3rd Battalion relieved the 2nd Battalion, 325th GIR, southeast of the Bois De Limors, and established contact with the 505th PIR on the right and 325th GIR on the left. The 2nd Battalion moved into reserve positions behind the 3rd Battalion, and the 1st Battalion took up positions behind the 3rd Battalion, 505th. The 1st Battalion took up positions in the rear of the 2nd. On 29 June the 1st Battalion relieved the 3rd Battalion, 505th, and became attached to the 505th. The 3rd Battalion was relieved by the 2nd Battalion, 507th attached, and moved into the 1st Battalion's former position on 30 July. The regiment patrolled actively along the front during the entire period.

82nd Airborne Artillery

The 319th Glider Field Artillery Battalion was in direct support of the 507th PIR, 320th Glider Field Artillery Battalion, in direct support of the 325th GIR, 456th Parachute Field Artillery Battalion, which in turn was in direct support of the 505th and 508th PIRs. The 87th Armored and 188th Field Artillery Battalions, attached, were in general support. The 319th Glider Field Artillery Battalion was placed in direct support of the 508th PIR on 24 June, and the 456th Parachute Field Artillery Battalion was placed in direct support of the 505th. During the remainder of the period support missions of the battalions were not changed, and Division Artillery continued to harass and interdict enemy troops and lines of communication.

80th Airborne Antiaircraft Battalion

Battery A was placed in support of the 505th. Battery B supported the 507th, and Battery C supported the 508th. The machine gun batteries D, E, and F provided antiaircraft protection for the Etienville and Vindefontaine Bridges.

307th Airborne Engineer Battalion

The Battalion during this period built roads through the Bois De Limors, checked the Division area for mines and booby traps, operated water points, made ground engineer reconnaissance, and screened the Etienville - Saint Jores Road to guard against observation from Hill 131. Squads from Company A guarded the bridges at Etienville and Vindefontaine.

Attached Troops

The 87th Armored and 188th Field Artillery Battalions remained attached to Division Artillery. Troop B, 4th Cavalry Reconnaissance Squadron, was relieved from attachment to the Division. Company A, 746th Tank Battalion, was relieved from attachment on 21 June. The 801st Tank Destroyer Battalion was attached on 30 June, and Company A, 607th Tank Destroyer Battalion, remained attached during the period. Company B, 87th Chemical Mortar Battalion, was relieved in the early part of the period.

D plus 25 to D plus 26, 1-2 July 1944

The Division continued to maintain positions in the Etienville Bridgehead with a front generally along the line as of D plus 14. Preparations were completed, reorganization effected, and new troops attached for the attack to the west on 3 July. The Division was firmly in contact with the 79th Infantry Division on the right and the 90th Infantry Division on the left. An Advance Division Command Post was opened at 2330 hours.

325th Glider Infantry Regiment

The regiment continued to hold position southwest of La Dranguerie, maintaining contact with the 508th PIR on the right and 507th on the left. The 1st Battalion remained on the right, 2nd Battalion on the left, and 3rd Battalion in reserve.

505th Parachute Infantry Regiment

The regiment continued to hold positions in the Bois de Limors, with the 1st Battalion, 508th PIR attached, on the left, and the 1st Battalion on the right. Patrolling continued. Contact was maintained with the 79th Infantry Division on the right and the 508th on the left.

507th Parachute Infantry Regiment

The regiment continued to hold positions in the vicinity of Pretot, maintaining contact with the 90th Infantry Division on the left and the 325th GIR on the right. The 1st Battalion held front line positions with the 3rd Battalion in reserve. The 2nd Battalion remained attached to the 508th PIR.

82nd Airborne Division Artillery

Preparations were made to displace and support the attack of the Division on 3 July. The 319th Glider Field Artillery Battalion remained in direct support of the 508th, the 320th Glider Field Artillery Battalion in direct support of the 325th Glider and 507th PIR, and the 456th Parachute Field Artillery Battalion in direct support of the 505th PIR. The 87th Armored Field Artillery Battalion, less Battery B, which reinforced the fire of the 320th, and the 188th Field Artillery Battalions were in general support. Company D, 86th Chemical Mortar Battalion (4,2 inch mortars), was placed under Division Artillery control and attached to the 505th PIR.

80th Airborne Antiaircraft Battalion

Batteries A and E were attached to the 505th PIR, Battery B to the 507th PIR, and Battery C to the 508th PIR for the 3 July attack.

307th Airborne Engineer Battalion

Two platoons of Company A were attached to the 325th GIR. One squad of Company B was attached to the 507th, and two squads from Company B were attached to each of the 505th and 508th PIRs. Squads of Company A guarding the bridges at Etienville and Vindefontaine were relieved by Corps engineers on 2 July.

Attached Troops

Company A, 712th Tank Battalion (attached to the Division), moved into the bridgehead area late on 2 July. The 1st Platoon was attached to the 507th, and the 2nd Platoon to the 325th GIR. The 801st Tank Destroyer Battalion was relieved from attachment on 1 July, and the 803rd Tank Destroyer Battalion was attached on 1 July at 0100 hours. Company A, 607th Tank Destroyer Battalion, remained attached. Company D, 86th Chemical Mortar Battalion, was attached at 1600 hours on 1 July and placed under control of the 82nd Division Artillery, and later was attached to the 505th PIR.

D plus 27, 3 July 1944

The Division attacked at 0630 after days of waiting, reorganization, and preparation, and despite heavy rainfall. The Division's mission was to attack, seize, and secure Hills 131 and 95 and the high ground northeast of La Haye Du Puits, known as the La Poterie Ridge. Flanked by the 79th Infantry Division on the right and the 90th Infantry Division on the left, the 82nd was to be pinched out of the VIII Corps attack and was to assemble and await further orders. The Division attacked according to plan, with the 505th PIR on the right, 508th PIR in the center, and the 325th GIR on the left. The 2nd Battalion 507th PIR initially covered a small draw between the 325th and 508th. Stubborn resistance was offered initially by the 265th and 353rd German Infantry Divisions reinforced by OST Battalions. The enemy had made good use of the 11 day delay to organize an elaborate defense. However, by aggressive action the Division moved ahead to seize Hill 131 by noon, and to secure the eastern edge of the Poterie Ridge, exclusive of the village of La Poterie, by dark. Fighting was sharp and severe, and enemy defensive positions were heavily mined and boody trapped. Many casualties were inflited on the enemy. The forward Division Command Post moved to Auvrairie.

325th Glider Infantry Regiment

With the 1st Battalion on the left and the 2nd Battalion on the right, the regiment jumped off at 0630 hours, meeting considerable small arms and mortar fire. In the vicinity of La Dranguerie the 3rd Battalion was commited temporarily to close a gap that had developed between the 2nd and 1st Battalions at 1000 hours. The 90th Infantry Division on the left flank was held up, leaving the flank exposed and under pressure. By 1600 hours the 325th had reached the town of Faudemer. At 1550 hours the regimental objective was changed from Hill 95 to the eastern edge of the La Poterie Ridge to include the village of La Poterie. The 2nd and 1st Battalions continued to attack towards the town, but increasing enemy opposition prevented the capture of the town by nightfall. The 3rd Battalion was again placed in the line, and the regiment dug in preparatory to attacking and seizing La Poterie the following day.

505th Parachute Infantry Regiment

The Regiment attacked at 0630 hours, initially with the 1st and 2nd Battalions in column, and the 2nd Battalion leading. Passing the creek line at Varenguebec, the 2nd Battalion seized Dupinerie Ridge (North of Hill 131) by 0830 hours and resumed the attack at 1015 hours, with the 1st Battalion abreast and on the right.. These two battalions, by bold advances, secured the north slope of Hill 131 and the Saint Sauveur Le Vicomte-La Haye Du Puits Highway by 1225 hours, despite heavy enemy artillery fire, mines, and booby traps. The 3rd Battalion followed the assault battalions to mop up by-passed pockets of resistance. The regimental zone was enlarged at 1550 hours to include all of Hill 131. The 3rd Battalion moved into position through the 2nd and into the 508th PIR's area on the southern slope of Hill 131. The regiment dug in by the end of the day along a line from La Sangsuriere south to Les Rouland, and then to a junction with the 508th at Blanchelande. Preparations were made to continue the attack on 4 July.

507th Parachute Infantry Regiment

The 2nd Battalion, under regimental control, attacked at 0630 hours, flanked on the left and right by the 325th GIR and 508th PIR, respectively. The Battalion cleared all enemies from its area and reached its objective (La Fauverie) by 1700. Preparations were then made to attack to the south the next day. Other units of the regiment remained in Division reserve south of Vindefontaine and prepared to follow the advance of the 325th GIR on Division order. The regiment moved to the vicinity of La Dranguerie at 1630. The 1st Battalion followed and maintained contact with the 325th, and the 3rd Battalion protected the Division's left flank to the left rear of the 1st Battalion.

508th Parachute Infantry Regiment

With the 2nd Battalion on the right and the 3rd Battalion on the left, the regiment attacked at 0630 hours, passing through the 1st Battalion's positions. The high ground between Varenguebec and La Dauderie was secured by 0900 hours, and the 1st Battalion moved into reserve in the vicinity of La Cotellerie. The 2nd Battalion reached the southern slope of Hill 131 by 1145 and was joined by the 3rd Battalion by 1600 hours. The regiment moved south at 2000 hours to occupy a zone in the vicinity of Blanchelande, dug in, and prepared to attack south towards the La Poterie Ridge. Enemy opposition was moderate to heavy during the action. Extensive minefields were encountered.

82nd Airborne Division Artillery

All batallions fired in preparation to precede the Division's attack, and during the entire action the battalions fired harassing, interdicion, and counter battery fire with telling effect, despite inclement weather, which precluded accurate observation. Reconnaissance was made to displace battalions into more favorable positions closer to the advancing infantry. A total of 7,727 rounds were fired during the period.

Attached Troops

One platoon of Company A, 712th Tank Battalion, supported the 325th GIR during its attack near La Dranguerie, and another platoon supported the 2nd Battalion, 507th PIR, in clearing its zone, then went into positions near La Fauverie commanding observation of the La Poterie-Pretot Highway. At 1315 one platoon of Company A, 803rd Tank Destroyer Battalion, moved to support the 2nd Battalion, 508th PIR. Company D, 86th Chemical Mortar Battalion, was relieved from attachment to the 505th PIR at 1920 hours and was attached to the 325th GIR.

D plus 26, 4 July 1944

The Division resumed its attack at 0800, and by the end of the day had secured Hill 95 and the La Poterie Ridge against a determined enemy. Many severe counterattacks were driven back, and any ground lost as a result of the counter thrusts was retaken. More than 500 enemy were killed and more than 700 taken prisoner in the bitter fighting.

325th Glider Infantry Regiment

The 1st and 3rd Battalions resumed the attack against the village of La Poterie at 0800 hours and secured it by 1250 hours. The 2nd Battalion remained in reserve. After passing through La Poterie the regiment occupied defensive positions within its sector and established contact with the 90th Infantry Division on the 82nd Airborne Division's left flank.

505th Parachute Infantry Regiment

The 1st and 3rd Battalions attacked at 0800 to seize the northern slope of Hill 95 and secured this objective by 1150 hours. Firm contact was made with adjacent units. Contact with the 3rd Battalion, 314th Infantry, 79th Infantry Division (on the right), was made at 2100 hours.

507th Parachute Infantry Regiment

The 2nd Battalion reverted to regimental control and moved at noon to the breakthrough position in the vicinity of Blanchelande. The 3rd Battalion moved into an assembly area north of La Poterie and attacked at 2015 hours through the 508th PIR to seize the western hill mass on La Poterie Ridge. The 3rd Battalion reached the hill and was consolidating positions and establishing contact with adjacent units by 2400 hours. The 2nd Battalion attacked at 2200 hours between the 2nd and the 3rd Battalions, 508th PIR, and pushed up to the center hill mass of La Poterie Ridge directly east of Hill 95. This Battalion circled the hill in the darkness against considerable small arms and artillery fire and prepared to seize it completely before daylight. The 1st Battalion, meanwhile, remained in position to the rear of the 325th GIR along the Division's right flank.

508th Parachute Infantry Regiment

At 0800 the Regiment attacked south against Hill 95 and the La Poterie Ridge. The 2nd Battalion, passing through elements of the 505th, seized Hill 95 at 1220. Enemy resistance was particulary strong, and losses were heavy on both sides. An enemy counterattack at 1400 hours forced the 2nd Battalion back, but it retook the position by 2400 hours, despite considerable artillery and small arms fire. The 3rd and 1st Battalions attacked at 0800 on the left of the regimental zone. Heavy concentrations of mortar, artillery, and small arms fire pinned the units down along the general line running due west from the village of La Poterie, and all attempts to reach the objective were repulsed during the day. The 2nd Battalion, 507th, moved into positions between the 2nd and 3rd Battalions, and launched an attack against the 3rd Battalion's objective at 2200. The 3rd Battalion, 507th, passed through elements of the 1st and 3rd Battalions in its attack at 2015 hours on the eastern edge and northern slopes of La Poterie Ridge.

82nd Airborne Division Artillery

Reinforced by eight battalions of VIII Corps artillery, the battalions of Division Artillery fired numerous concentrations in support of the infantry advance, and succeeded in breaking up enemy counterattack in the vicinity of Hill 95 and along the La Poterie Ridge.

Attached Troops

Company D, 86th Chemical Mortar Battalion, was relieved from attachment to the Division at 2300 hours. Company A, 607th Tank Destroyer Battalion, was relieved at 1115 hours. One platoon of tanks from Company A, 712th Tank Battalion, was relieved from the 325th and supported the 508th in repulsing counterattacks in that setor. Guns from the 803rd Tank Destroyer Battalion were placed on the south slope of Hill 131 to maintain fire on the woods south and west of the 508th front.

D plus 29, 5 July 1944

The Division secured all of the area within its zone of action, mopping up all remaining pockets of enemy resistance, consolidating defensive positions, and maintaining contact with the adjacent units in their advance to pinch off the Division. Corps orders restrained the Division from further advances. Defensive positions were established along the general line from Hill 131 south along the Saint Sauveur Le Vicomte-La Haye Du Puits Highway, to the southern slopes of Hill 95, and thence along the southern slope of the La Poterie Ridge.

325th Glider Infantry Regiment
The regiment established a defensive line on the forward slopes of the La Poterie Ridge with the 3rd Battalion, 507th attached, on the regiment's right flank. Contact was maintained with the advancing 90th Infantry Division on the left.

505th Parachute Infantry Regiment
The regiment maintained defensive positions on the reserve slope of Hill 95, and from that point north to the base of Hill 131. Contact was maintained with the 79th Infantry Division on the right and the 508th PIR.

507th Parachute Infantry Regiment
The 2nd Battalion continued fighting to secure the westernmost hill of the La Poterie Ridge due east from Hill 95. This ridge was under control at 0700 hours. During the remainder of the day this battalion killed or destroyed all enemy within its area, established contact with adjacent units, and strengthened positions. The 3rd Battalion secured the easternmost hill of the La Poterie Ridge and was attached to the 325th GIR after having established contact. The 1st Battalion remained in reserve.

508th Parachute Infantry Regiment
The 1st Battalion moved into reserve positions in the vicinity of Blanchelande. The 2nd Battalion cleared enemy from the forward slopes of Hill 131 and maintained contact with the 505th. The 3rd Battalion, in the center of La Poterie Ridge, established defensive positions between the 2nd Battalion, 507th, and the 2nd Battalion on Hill 131. The regiment suffered from concentrated enemy artillery fire. All enemy were cleared from the regiment sector.

Captain William Nation, Service Co, 508th PIR
Letter to his parents:

Dear Folks,

On the fourth all guns were supposed to have shot a salvo in memory of our regular fourth of July, but from where I stood, you couldn't tell who might be celebrating—dodging 88s and heavier artillery, and from listening to our own whiz over our heads all day, it was a noisy and heated fourth. From now on, I'll be content with no loud noise on that day. Three artillery shells hit within 20 to 40 yards from me this week, and not a thing touched me. The only thing I felt was the tingling and electrifying feeling it left in my mouth and heat. They were bad shots. These hynies will shoot at just one man with one of those things, and they shoot so fast and hard that you can't get cover before they are on you.

If the roses and flowers can still bloom and blossom in the midst of ruins, craters, and charred debris, then surely I can smile through it all and be as cheerful as I know how...." (Author's Note: Captain Nation served with the 508th throughout the Fall of that year and into the next, participating in the Market Garden Operation and in the Battle of the Bulge, until he was killed in action in the early morning hours of 31 January 1945 while setting up a forward CP near Lanzerath, Belgium.)

82nd Airborne Division Artillery
All battalions assisted in breaking up an enemy counterattack, particulary in the 507th PIR area. The 456th Parachute Field Artillery Battalion was ordered to reinforce fires of the 319th Glider Field Artillery Battalion, which was still in direct support of the 508th PIR. Ammunition expended during the day totalled 2,733 rounds.

D plus 30 to D plus 31, 6 -7 July 1944

The Division maintained and strengthened defensive positions, drove out all attempts by the enemy to infiltrate patrols through the sector, and maintained contact with the 79th Infantry Division on the right and the 90th Infantry Division on the left. The 2nd Battalion, 325th GIR, moved into position between the 2nd and the 3rd Battalions, 507th. The 505th PIR sector was enlarged to include the eastern slopes of Hill 95 and, with the 2nd Battalion, 508th, attacked and cleared the area of infiltrating enemy patrols. At 0800 on 7 July the Division regrouped its forces, placing the 325th GIR and 508th PIR in reserve and making the 505th and 507th PIRs responsible for the right and left portions, respectively, of the Division's front lines.

D plus 32 to D plus 35, 8 – 11 July 1944

The Division reverted to Corps reserve and was relieved of all attachments. The 8th Infantry Division passed through the Division's positions to continue the attack to the south on 8 July, D plus 32. The Division assembled, and on 11 July withdrew into First Army reserve. It then moved to Utah Beach preparatory to its return to base camps in England.

Upon returning to base camps the Division immediately began an intensive training program. The Division had not received reinforcements in France, and the Infantry losses were particulary heavy, one company coming out of the lines with a strength of only sixteen officers and enlisted men.

Refitting also occupied much of the time, however, by mid-August this phase had been accomplished, and training dominated the activities. One phase of the training included tests to determine the possibilities of employing heavy bombers in air landing operations. Both the B-17 and B-24 were used in these tests.

Major General Matthew B. Ridgway left the Division to become Commanding General of the XVIII Corps (Airborne), and Brigadier General James Gavin assumed command of the 82nd Airborne Division.

As the month of August ended the Division was moving to takeoff airfields in the British Midlands in preparation for a mission in Belgium that was canceled less than 24 hours prior to scheduled takeoff time. The Division's next mission began 17 September when it jumped and glided into the Nijmegen - Grave - Groesbeek area of the Netherlands.

Lt. Colonel Benjamin Vandervoort, 2/505th PIR.

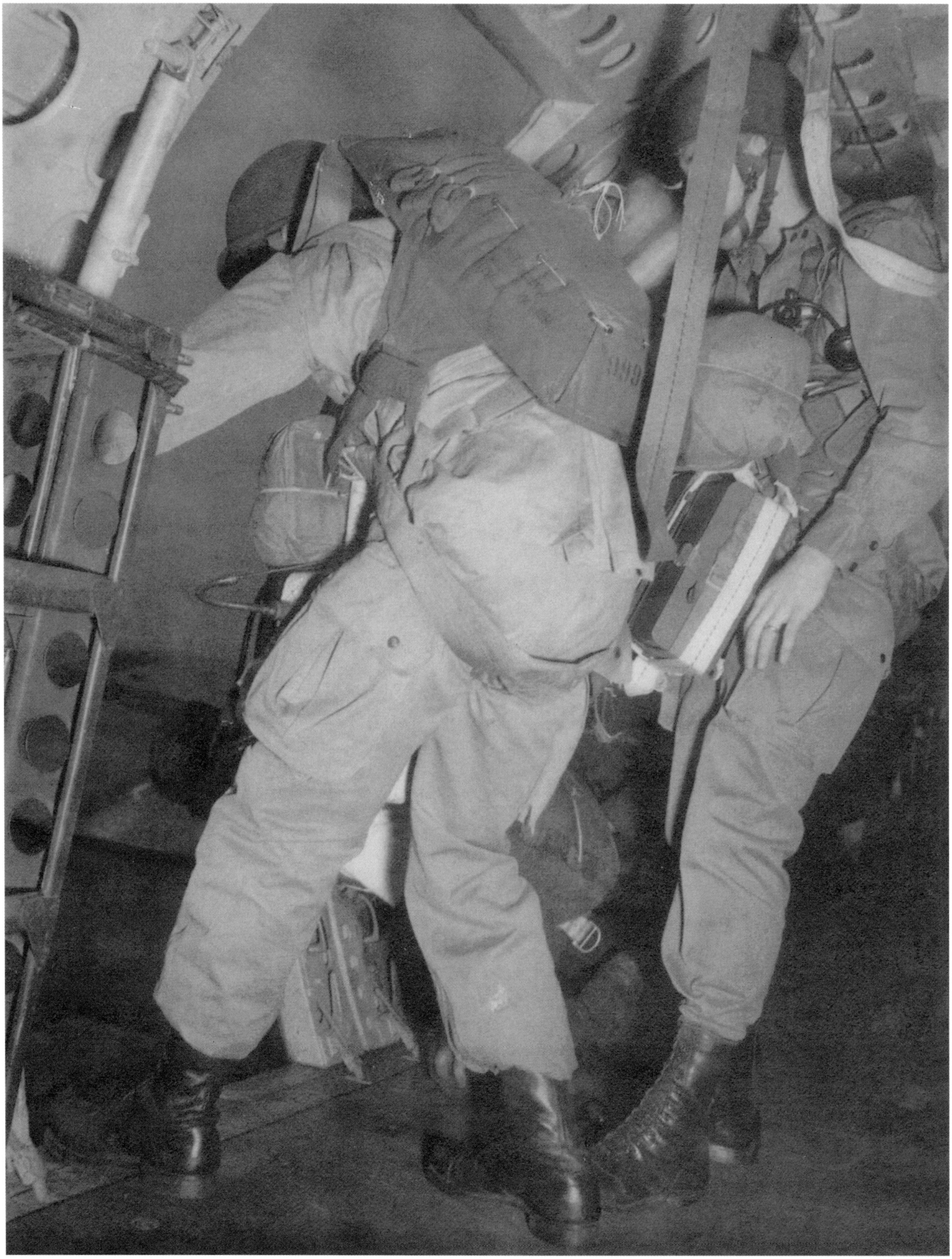

A demolition platoon of the 507th PIR during a training jump at Fort Benning.

General Matthew Ridgway, commanding the 82nd Airborne Division.

These two paratroopers of the 508th PIR are ready to board for Operation Neptune.

These two 508th PIR paratroopers carry a Griswold Bag for their guns and a T-5 parachute.

A few minutes before boarding the C-47.

A stick of the 508th PIR.

June 5, 1944, these two paratroopers of the 508th are about to embark: destination, Normandy.

One last coffee cup before the great departure for these 508th PIR paratroopers.

505th PIR Pathfinders, 3rd Team.

505th PIR Pathfinders, 2nd Team.

505th PIR Pathfinders, 1st Team.

507th PIR Pathfinders, 3rd Team.

507th PIR Pathfinders, 2nd Team.

507th PIR Pathfinders, 1st Team.

508th PIR Pathfinders, 3rd Team, 2nd Lt. Gene Williams.

508th PIR Pathfinders, 2nd Team, Lt. Charles R.Gaudio

508th PIR Pathfinders, 1st Team, .2nd Lt. Robert J. Weaver

A bulldozer leaves a Waco glider on the LZ.

A Horsa Glider in a landing field in Normandy on D-Day.

A Horsa Glider in a hedgerow in Normandy, in the Fresville area.

Dead American glidermen laid in front of their crashed Horsa Glider on D-Day.

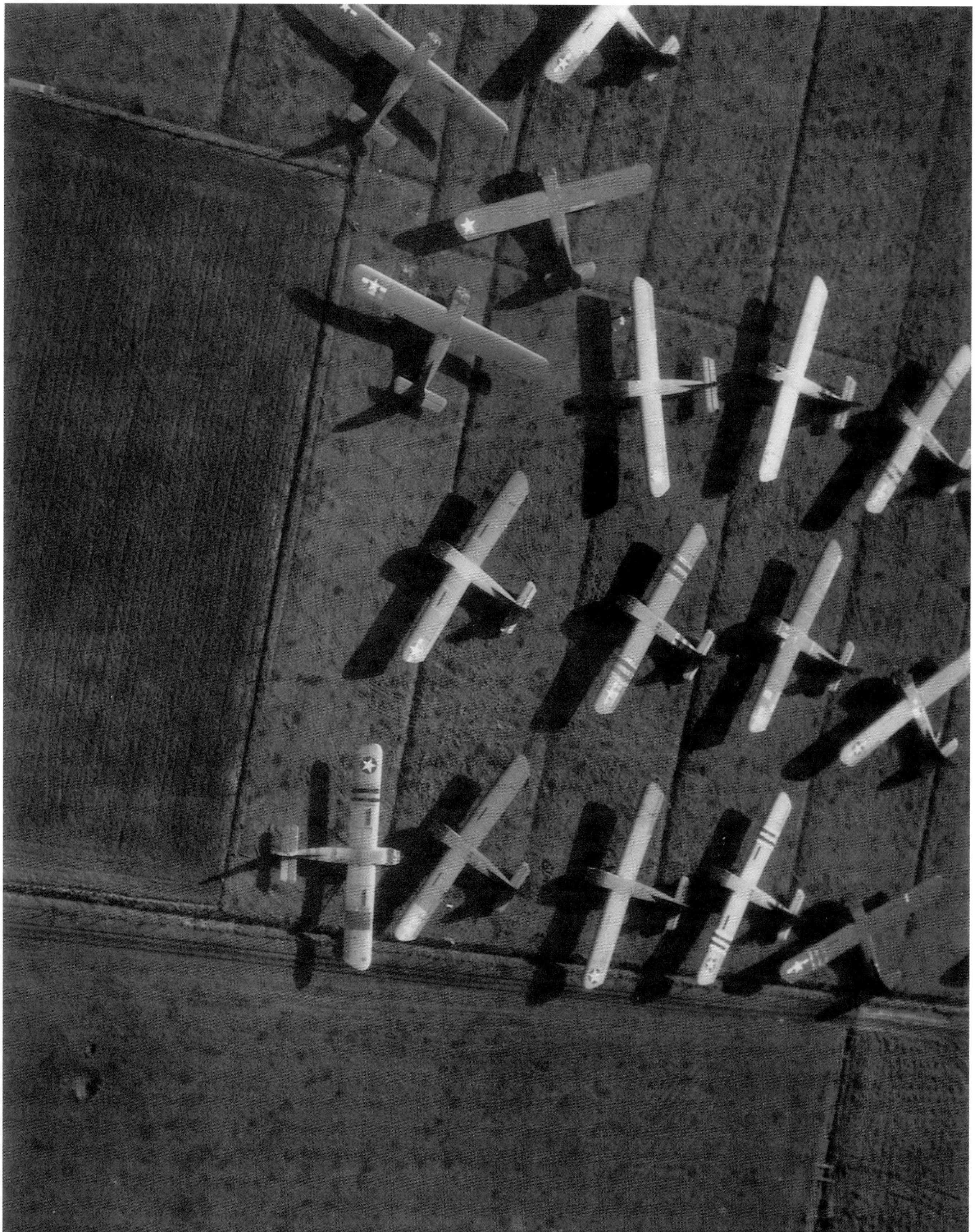

The Waco CG-4A gliders are assembled on airfields in England before being taken by C-47s to Normandy.

Upon landing many gliders were damaged by the hedgerows of Normandy.

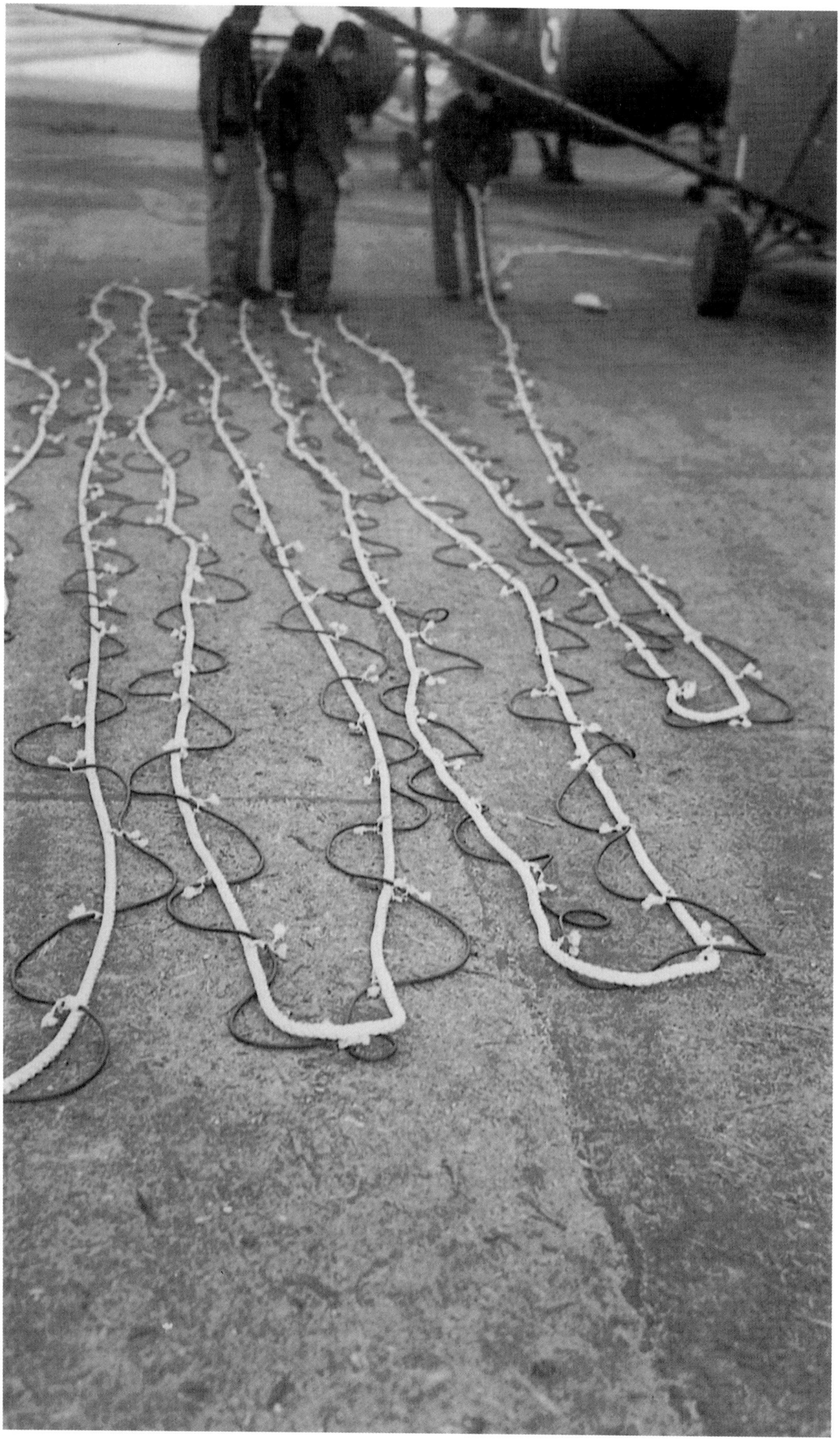

In this photograph, both parts of a Waco glider traction cable can be seen. The electrical wire is a radio wire that allows the pilot of the glider to talk to the pilots of the plane.

The Waco CG-4A glider with its invasion painting, before the Neptune Operation.

The designers of the Waco CG-4 glider envisioned it landing in relatively sedate liaison on airstrips or meadows clear of obstructions, not smashing through fences, hedgerows, and earthen embankments. To reinforce the nose and reduce damage to the crew, the Griswold Nose "Cowcatcher" was devised. Only a few were available for Neptune.

Over 16,000 of the Waco CG-4A gliders were made during the war.

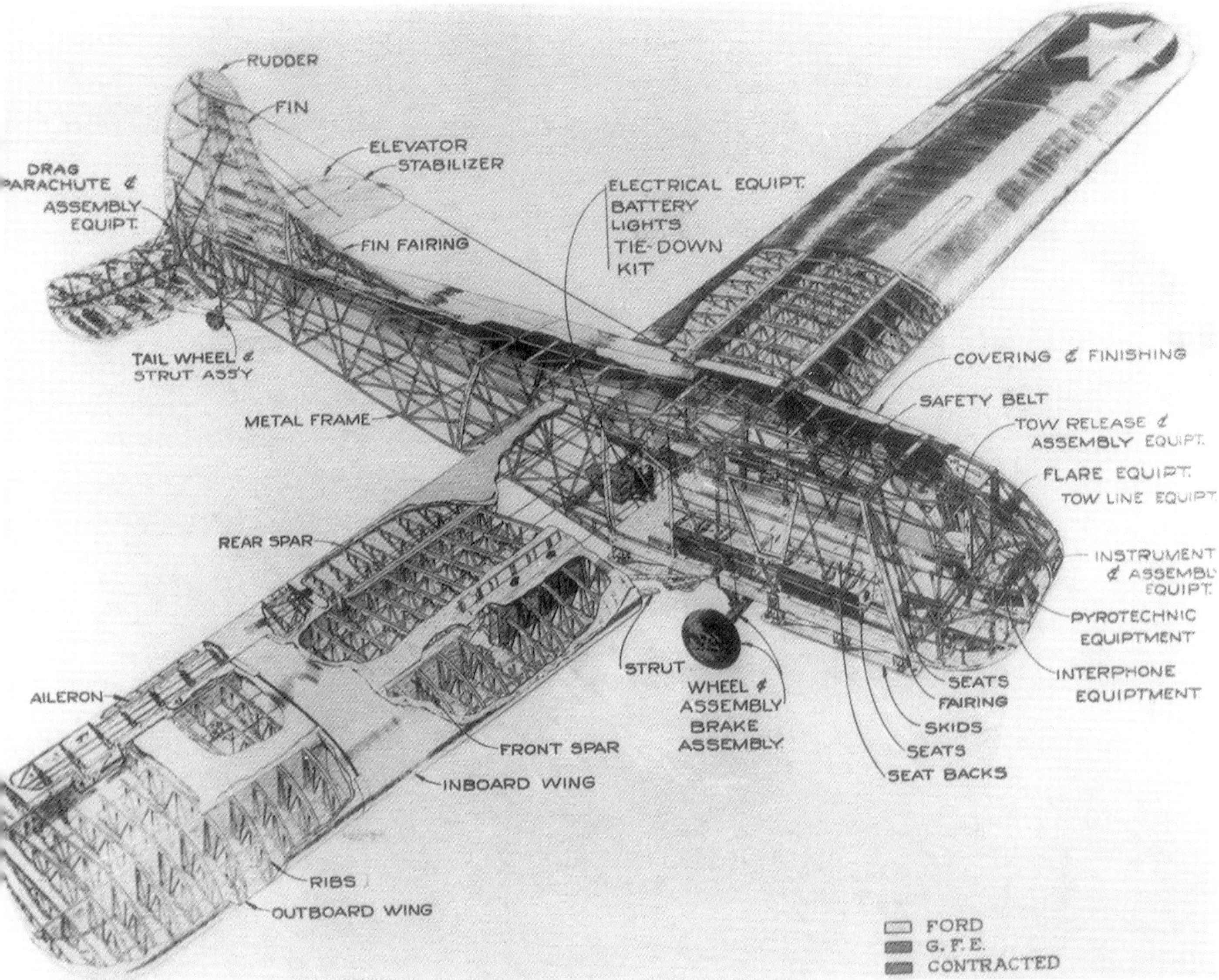

Over 70,000 parts are necessary to build a Waco glider.

These soldiers of the 325th GIR are searching the remains of a Waco during the Market Garden Operation.

The transportation of soldiers by glider was a new war concept that had never been used before by the U.S. Army.

A British Horsa glider, damaged on landing, will be burned later on.

A Waco CG-4 glider upon exiting the assembly workshops in England.

Crash of a C-47 near Chef du Pont.

Paratrooper of the 508th PIR who just received his paratrooper certificate.

James McCallum of the 505th PIR participated in four jumps for the 505th in Sicily, Italy, Normandy, and Holland.

General James Gavin.

Top: A paratrooper killed in action in the vicinity of Sainte Mere Eglise. Bottom: The first paratroopers of the 505th with German horses in Sainte Mere Eglise.

Drop of a bundle in Normandy.

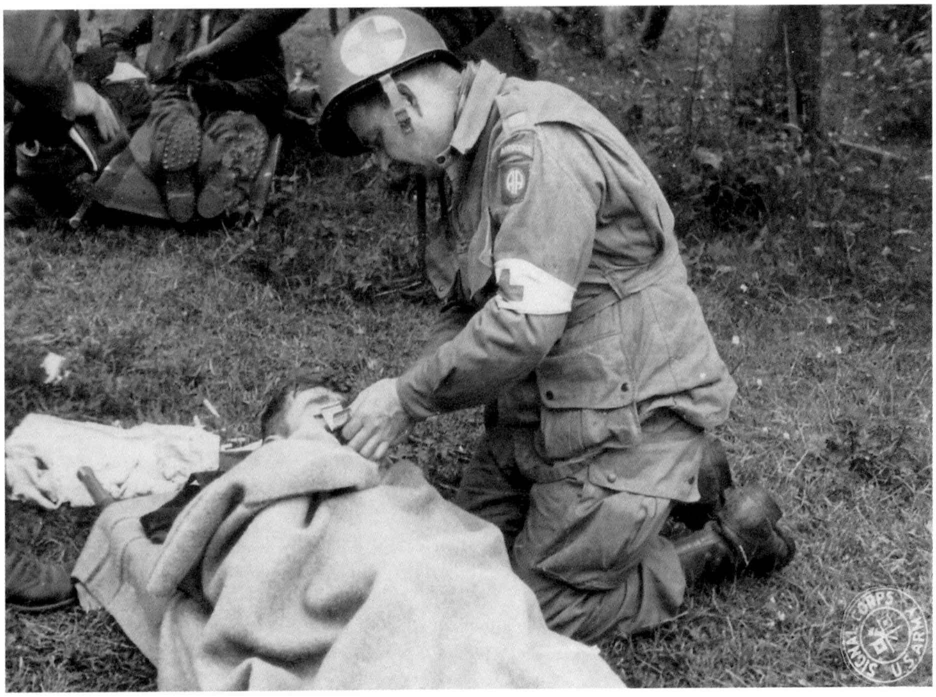

A medic of the 505th with a German wounded waiting for evacuation to a medical station at Utah Beach.

A 505th trooper uses a captured horse in Sainte Mere Eglise.

A 505th Trooper leaves Sainte Mere Eglise with French civilians.

Main Street of Sainte Mere Eglise after the battle.

A 505th trooper with French civilians in Sainte Mere Eglise.

Sainte Mere Eglise post card, at the beginning of the century.

Sainte Mere Eglise post card.

German Headquarters at Sainte Mere Eglise (Fauville).

Main Street Sainte Mere Eglise at the beginning of the century.

Sainte Mere Eglise Post card at the beginning of the century.

Colonel Ekman (in the center), commanding officer of the 505th PIR.

Sainte Mere Eglise.

Colonel Ekman's (505th PIR) last jump in Germany.

Sainte Mere Eglise.

Sainte Mere Eglise.

Sainte Mere Eglise church.

Sainte Mere Eglise church before the war.

Above and following: A medic with a German wounded.

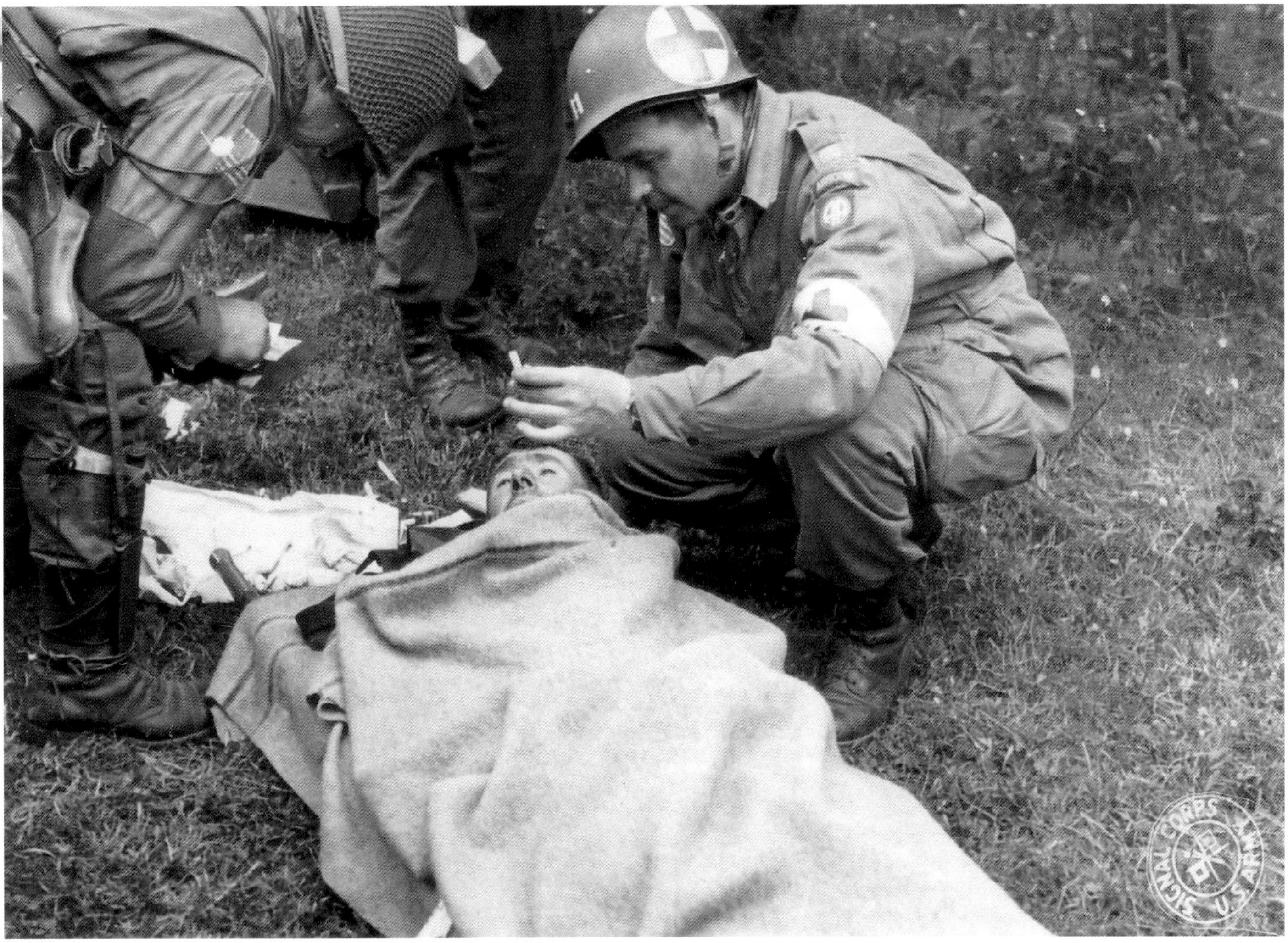
SIGNAL CORPS
U.S. ARMY

Sgt. George Leidenheimer of the 507th PIR joined the 17th Airborne Division with his Regiment after the Normandy Campaign.

OB. Hill as a young paratrooper in 1942.

Lt. Malcolm Brannen (Hq Co/508th) killed German General Falley.

Lt. Malcolm Brannen.

Lt. Malcolm Brannen in Nottingham, England, before D-Day.

Bernaville Castle in Picauville before the War. It was General Falley's HQ, who was killed on June 6, 1944, by 508th PIR Lt. Malcolm Brannen and his men.

A temporary cemetery is set out on a field near Sainte Mere Eglise.

General Wilhelm Falley, Commanding the 91st German Infantry Division. Killed on June 6, 1944, by Lt. Malcolm Brannen of the 508th PIR.

A German tank destroyed near Sainte Mere Eglise.

First paratroopers in Sainte Mere Eglise with German captured horses on June 7th.

CO.K 325th Glider Infantry Regiment at Epinal, France.

Henry Joseph Hirleman, Co.I 325th GIR, was a Pathfinder in Holland.

Captain Robert Piper 505th PIR.

Chaplain George Wood, 505th PIR, outside the Sainte Mere Eglise Aid Station.

At the end of the Normandy campaign, Captain Paul Smith of the 507th PIR had just received his rank of Major from Colonel Edson Raff, new Commanding Officer. Note that Smith is still wearing his rank of Captain on his A2 jacket.

Glider pilots back in England, 8 June.

Two Medics of the 507th PIR at the end of the Battle of La Fiére.

Back in England.

The Mayor of a French village greeting the Officers of the 507th PIR.

Captain Paul Smith of the 507th PIR, during the Campaign, was isolated with a group of paratroopers for several days in the Amfreville swamps.

Joe Lizut of the 508th PIR during the engagements in Normandy.

These young French children met the first American paratrooper.

Above and following: 82nd elements arrived in Saint Marcouf on June 6th.

SIGNAL CORPS
U.S. ARMY

Paratroopers arrive in Saint Marcouf.

Left to Right: Henry Joseph Hirlemann and Russel Andermann (Both men served in Company I, 325th Glider Infantry Regiment). Russel Andermannn was one who made the charge of the La Fiere causeway in Normandy. Hirlermann was a Pathfinder in Holland.

These two 508th PIR paratroopers have the features of those who have lived difficult moments. This picture was taken in the Chef du Pont area.

Two soldiers of the 508th in Normandy. The one on the left wears a Field Jacket 41 and carries a U.S. M1A1 rifle.

La Fiere Bridge post war post card.

La Fiere Manor house on June 9th, after the battle.

Pvt. Marcus Heim of the 505th PIR.

Captain Morgan Brakonecke of the 507th PIR.

Sgt. Carl Letson of the 507th PIR. He jumped far from his Drop Zone in Normandy and ended the war as a POW in Germany.

Lt. King (508th PIR), KIA in Normandy a few days later.

Lt. Colonel Mendez (3rd Bn/508th) on the left with two officers of his battalion (Major Bell on right).

Lt. Colonel Louis Mendez with his driver.

Colonel Louis Mendez after WWII.

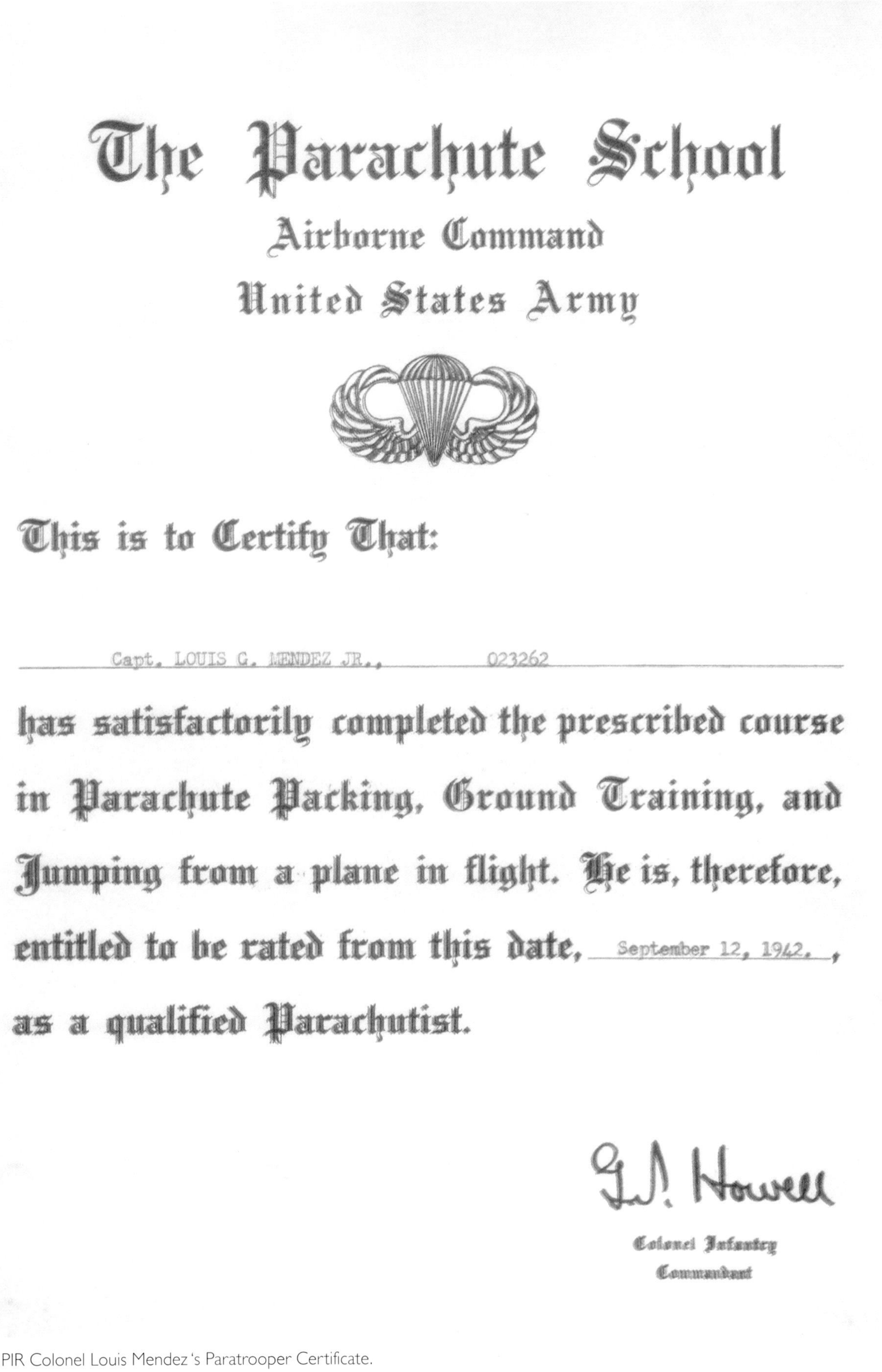

The Parachute School
Airborne Command
United States Army

This is to Certify That:

Capt. LOUIS G. MENDEZ JR., 023262

has satisfactorily completed the prescribed course in Parachute Packing, Ground Training, and Jumping from a plane in flight. He is, therefore, entitled to be rated from this date, September 12, 1942., as a qualified Parachutist.

G. P. Howell

Colonel Infantry
Commandant

508th PIR Colonel Louis Mendez's Paratrooper Certificate.

Above: Dog tags and shoulder flag worn by Colonel Louis Mendez during D-Day. Below: A few memorabilia items belonging to Colonel Louis Mendez, and kept by his family.

Lt. Thomas Shanley at Fort Benning in 1941.

Thomas Shanley as a cadet of the Military Academy of West Point.

Lt.Colonel Thomas Shanley in 1943.

Pvt. Irwing Shanley of the 508th PIR.

Major Gordon Smith, 507th PIR, at Fort Benning, 1943.

Major Gordon Smith in a German Hospital in Rennes with two officers of the 101st Abn. Div and a British POW.

Lt. Gordon Smith, a young officer of the 501st Parachute Battalion. His uniform is the special "balloon cloth" jumpsuit recently adopted and worn through 1941 by the 501st Para Bn.

Parachute packing tables at Fort Benning in 1941. At the time, paratroopers packed their own parachutes.

A few members of the 507th PIR basketball team. Major Gordon Smith is the second on the left.

Major Gordon Smith. He just received his new M42 jumping outfit and proudly displays his Colt 45.

Robert White, 508th PIR.

Lt. Lester W. Pollom, HQ CO, 508th PIR.

Pvt. George Strenkle, 508th PIR.

George Strenkle, day before D-Day, ready to board the plane.

Jack Schlegel (508th PIR) top right with Gen. Wilhelm falley's Headquarter's flag.

Lt. Bodack was wounded in Normandy.

Sgt. Jack Schlegel (3/508th PIR) in 1945. He wears the British Paratrooper wings on his right sleeve.

Cpl. Jack Schlegel in 1943.

All ex-POWs of the 508th who escaped during WWII; Schlegel is in the first row.

A 325th trooper in Neuville au Plain.

Ed Rokosz, 508th PIR.

Captain Chet Graham of the 508th PIR on a German motorbike on Hill 30, where he fought with Lt. Colonel Shanley.

After the Battle of La Fiere, the German vehicles are gathered in a field.

A German halftrack destroyed during the Battle of La Fiere.

Captain Robert Rae before a training jump at Fort Benning.

Captain Robert Rae (2nd left) of the 507th PIR right before a training jump.

Young Lt. Robert Rae at Fort Benning. A few months later, he would become the hero of the Battle of La Fiere.

Robert White of the 508th is looking at the german sniper he has just killed (Note two bullets holes through his right sleeve under flag).

Sgt. Frank Staples of the 508th PIR, during the crossing of the Atlantic Ocean in early 1944.

Sgt. Frank Staples and Pvt. Barton of the 508th PIR Company D.

Sgt. Frank Staples. He is carrying his dismantled Garand rifle in the Griswold Bag.

508th paratroopers a few minutes after the battle of Baupte.

A C-47 crash in the swamps near the Merderet River in the Picauville area.

S.R. Hartline, 325th GIR.

The 325th is engaged in the battle for Ham station.

Cpl. Walter Choquette (507th PIR), who was murdered at Graignes June 10, 1944.

Capt. Frank Naughton during the Battle of the Bulge; he was in Graignes during the Normandy campaign.

Certificate of Frank naughton.

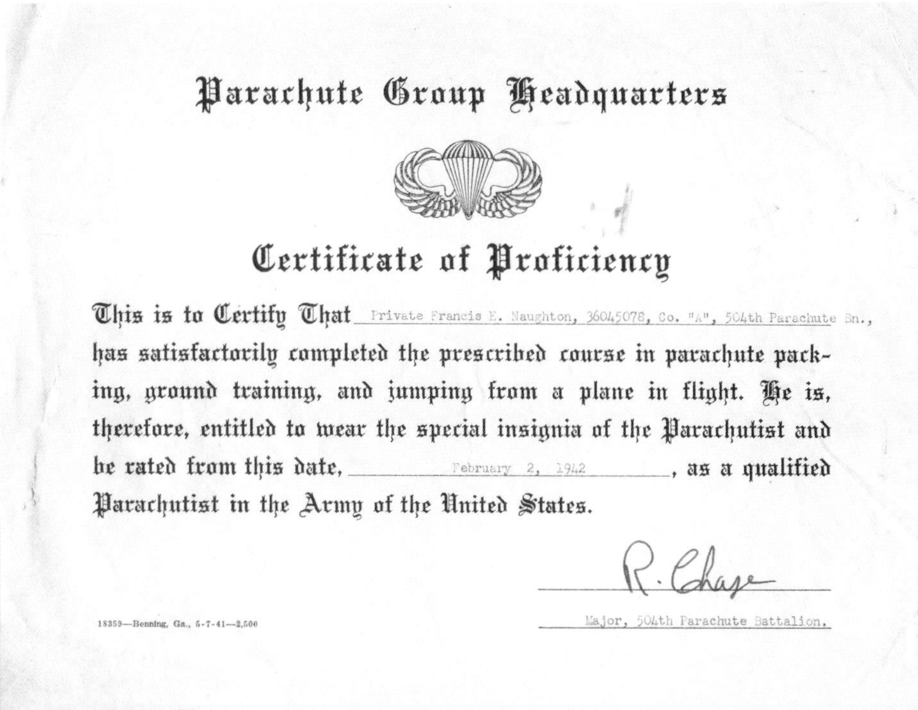

Parachute Group Headquarters

Certificate of Proficiency

This is to Certify That Private Francis E. Naughton, 36045078, Co. "A", 504th Parachute Bn., has satisfactorily completed the prescribed course in parachute packing, ground training, and jumping from a plane in flight. He is, therefore, entitled to wear the special insignia of the Parachutist and be rated from this date, February 2, 1942, as a qualified Parachutist in the Army of the United States.

R. Chase

Major, 504th Parachute Battalion.

18359—Benning, Ga., 5-7-41—2,500

Frank Naughton's first jump at Fort Benning in 1942.

Captain David Brummit (S-3, 507th PIR); he fought at Graignes.

A German SS killed in the vicinity of Graignes.

Sgt. George Hinchliff of the 507th PIR landed in Graignes, over 20 miles away from his DZ, and fought for several days with his company against the SS of the 17th SS Panzer-Grenadier Division "Götz Von Berlichingen."

Lt. Frank Naughton of the 507th PIR is receiving his rank of Captain from Colonel Edson Raff at the end of the Battle of Normandy.

These three Germans were killed by a 325th platoon during the Battle of Le Ham.

A group of paratroopers of the 508th PIR HQ Co. OB. Hill is the second on the right. He lost his rank as sergeant as well as a tooth in a fight with an officer of his company. The photograph was taken in Frankfurt, Germany, in July 1945.

Crash of a Waco glider into a farm roof. The pilot is in the foreground.

Lou Horn of the 507th PIR participated in the Campaign of Normandy, the Battle of the Bulge, and the Varsity Operation with the 507th PIR; he finished the war with the 505th PIR in Germany.

Lou Horn left the 507th and joined the 505th after being wounded.

Troopers of the 325th in Etienville; the barn on the left was a First Aid station.

325th in Etienville.

Two German Paratroopers killed near Saint Come du Mont.

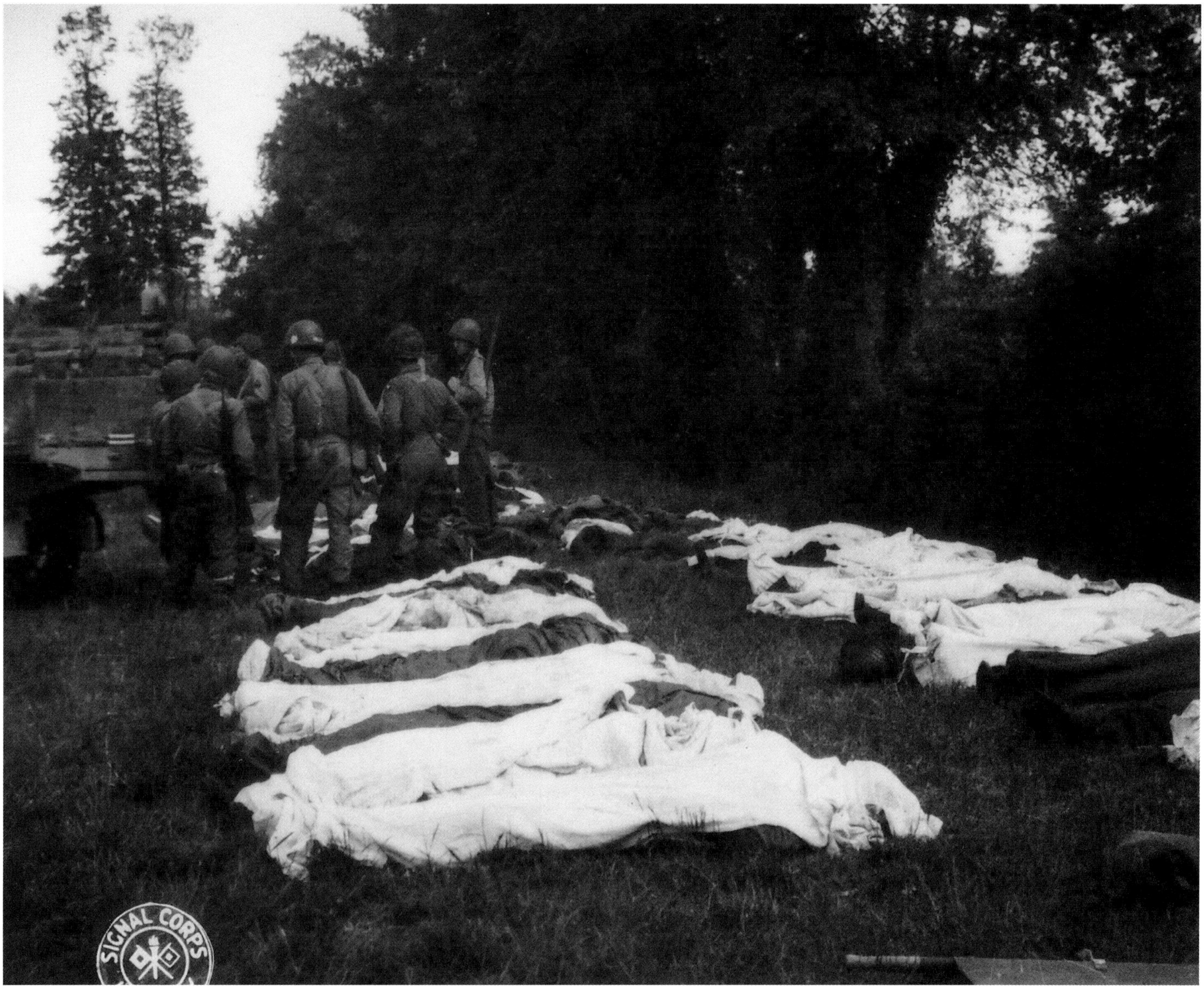

A temporary cemetery is set out on a field near Sainte Mere Eglise.

German bodies are unloaded from a truck by French civilians.

82nd Abn. Div.First Aid Station in the vicinity of Blosville.

Hill 95.

These 508th PIR soldiers are resting shortly before resuming their advance.

An 82nd Airborne Division trooper in the fields and hedgerows of Normandy.

A group of paratroopers of the 508th PIR Company D has found a ditch to spend the night, in the area of Hill 95.

Despite the wounds to his arm, this paratrooper keeps his spirits high.

These two 508th PIR paratroopers are taking a break in a ditch.

2/505th PIR in Saint Sauveur le Vicomte; Lt. Col. Benjamin Vandervoort is in the center with a crutch.

2/505th in Saint Sauveur Le Vicomte.

A German Command Car destroyed near Saint Saouveur Le Vicomte.

Lt. Chris Heisler of the 507th PIR. His plane was shot down during the jump in Normandy. However, he had time to jump with his stick, but lost many men during the jump. Captured shortly after landing, he finished the war in an Oflag in Germany.

Pvt. Jack Summers of the 507th PIR.

These soldiers of the 507th PIR are advancing cautiously in the Etienville area.

Above and following: Medics of the 507th PIR are carrying some wounded in the Pont L'Abbé-Etienville area.

Above and following: The Bon Sauveur Psychiatry Hospital at Picauville was damaged during the fighting and the patients had to leave.

A paratrooper of the 507th PIR among the ruins of the Picauville hospital.

General Gavin (on the right) talking to one of his officers.

General James Gavin armed with a Garand M1 rifle.

Two officers of the 82nd Airborne Division take stock of the situation during the fighting in the hedgerows.

Paratroopers of the 507th PIR are advancing on a Normandy road in the Amfreville area.

Each house is carefully searched, for a sniper may be hiding inside.

Young Normandy children admiring the paratroopers of the 82nd Airborne Division.

Normandy civilians helped the paratroopers by giving information about enemy positions and providing foods and Calvados liquor.

Above and following: The paratroopers of the 82nd Airborne Division crossing many Normandy villages amid the joyful cheers of the Normandy people, who are regaining their freedom after four years of German occupation.

RESTAURANT

The junction with the first elements of the force that disembarked at Utah Beach.

This soldier of the 325th GIR heads towards Amfreville, after the engagements of La Fiere.

The first vehicles of the Division arrived at Utah Beach by gliders, and the heaviest with the Seaborne assault.

A wounded paratrooper of the 508th waiting for his evacuation on Utah Beach.

These paratroopers are waiting for their evacuation to England on Utah Beach.

Exhausted, these 508th paratroopers fell into a ditch.

This 508th paratrooper proudly displays a German coat taken from the enemy he just killed.

Pvt. Frank Mc Kee of the 508th PIR at Camp Blanding, Florida.

A group of paratroopers of both airborne divisions, dropped far away from their Drop Zone. On the left, Captain Hawkins of the 456th Parachute Field Artillery of the 82nd Airborne Division. Photo taken by a member of the French Resistance in the Quettehou area.

This 508th PIR paratrooper has been wounded during the fighting in Normandy.

The fighting in the hedgerows is worse than fighting in the jungle.

Pvt. Gail Sauer of the 507th PIR in Northern Ireland in January 1943.

Pvt. Ed Jezioski of the 507th PIR back in England after jumping in Normandy. He participated in the Battle of La Fiere.

This paratrooper of the 82nd Airborne will be jumping soon in Normandy with his bazooka.

Captain Simons of the 508th. He was killed during the assault of Hill 95 in July 1944.

A 508th trooper in a hedgerow of Normandy.

A 508th trooper in Normandy.

Sgt. Bill How (Supply NCO) 3rd Bn, 508th PIR.

When the shooting stopped around La Haye Du Puits, First Army Commander Omar Bradley stopped by to present decorations to the 82nd Abn Division. Leftmost is Lt. Col. Krause, with Lt. Col. Vandervoort facing Bradley, then Capt. Rae (507th PIR), two medics, then Marcus Heim (1st Bn/505th PIR).

Captain William Nation's Memorabilia.

Captain William Nation at Camp Blanding, Florida, in 1942.

Captain William Nation, Service Co, 508th PIR.

508th Parachute Infantry
Regiment
United States Army

This is to Certify That:

CAPTAIN WILLIAM H. NATION 0-1287569

has satisfactorily completed the prescribed course in Parachute Packing, Ground Training, and has made the required number of Parachute Jumps from a plane in flight. He is, therefore, rated from this date 14 August 1942 as a qualified Parachutist

Ray E. Lindquist

Colonel, 508th Parachute Infantry
Commanding

Certificate of Captain William Nation

First cimetery near Sainte Mere Eglise.

First ceremony at the cemetery of Sainte Mere Eglise.

Chaplain Francis L. Sampson gives absolution to paratroopers killed in action.

Two French women place flowers on a paratrooper's grave.

Painting of General Gavin.

A detachment of the 508th, representing the 82nd Airborne Division at Sainte Mere Eglise, June 6, 1946, for acceptance of the croix de Guerre for units of the 82nd, including the 508th. General Le Gentilhomme presents individual awards of the Croix de Guerre.

Marlene Dietrich. In a few months she became the 82nd Airborne Division's Godmother, and kept a love relationship with General Gavin.

After the Normandy campaign, the 507th was transferred to the 17th Airborne Division. From now on, these paratroopers wear the "talon topic" patch.

Stella to the glory of the 82nd Airborne Division at Fort Benning.

Iron Mike Monument at Sainte Mere L'Eglise that overlooks La Fiere Causeway and the Merderet River.

Monument of the 507th PIR at Amfreville inaugurated on July 23, 2002.

At the end of the War, the 82nd Airborne Division parades in big American cities.

Appendix I: Command During the 82nd Airborne Division's Participation in the Normandy Campaign

Commanding General: Major General Matthew B. Ridgway
Assistant Commanding General: Brigadier General James M. Gavin
Assistant Commanding General: Brigadier General George P. Howell

325th Glider Infantry Regiment: Colonel Harry L. Lewis
1/325: Lt.Colonel Klemm R. Boyd
2/325: John H. Swenson
3/325: Lt. Colonel Charles A. Carrell

504th Parachute Infantry Regiment*: Colonel Reuben H. Turner

505th Parachute Infantry Regiment: Colonel William E. Ekman
1/505: Major Frederick C.A Kellam
2/505: Lt.Colonel Benjamin H. Vandervoort
3/505: Lt.Colonel Edward C. Krause

507th Parachute Infantry Regiment: Colonel George V. Millet (captured by enemy on or about 8 June 1944)
Lieutenant Colonel Arthur A. Maloney (from o/a 8 june)
Colonel Edson D. Raff (from 15 June 1944)
1/507: Lt.Colonel Edwin J. Ostberg
2/507: Lt.Colonel Charles Timmes
3/507: Lt. Colonel Willliam A. Kuhn

508th Parachute Infantry Regiment: Colonel Roy E. Lindquist
1/508: Lt.Colonel Batcheller (Killed 6 June 1944)
2/508: Lt.Colonel Thomas Shanley
3/508: Lt.Colonel Louis G. Mendez

Pathfinders: Major Neal L. Roberts

82nd Airborne Division Artillery: Colonel Francis A. March
319th Glider Field Artillery Battalion: Lt. Colonel James C. Todd
320th Glider Field Artillery Battalion: Lt. Colonel Paul. E. Wright
376th Parachute Field Artillery Battalion: Lieutenant Colonel Wilbur M. Griffith
456th Parachute Field Artillery Battalion: Lt. Colonel Wagner J. D'Alessio
80th Airborne Antiaircraft Battalion: Lt. Colonel Raymond E. Singleton
307th Airborne Engineer Battalion (less CO.C): Lt. Colonel Robert S. Palmer (captured by enemy on or about 6 June)
Major Edwin A Bedell (from 8 June 1944)
307th Airborne Medical Company: Major William H. Houston (killed 6 June 1944)
Major Jerry J. Beldew (from 6 June 1944)
407th Airborne Quatermaster Company: Captain Samuel H. Mays
782nd Airborne Ordnance Maintenance Company: Capt. Jeff; Davis Jr.
82nd Airborne Division Headquarters Company: Capt. George J. Claussen
82nd Airborne Signal Company: First Lieutenant Robert B. Nerf
82nd Airborne Reconnaissance Platoon: First Lieutenant Joseph V. Demasi
82nd Airborne Military Ploice Platoon: Major Frederick G. Mc Collum
82nd Parachute Maintenance Company: Captain James E. Griffin

*During Normandy Operation remained in base camps in the United Kingdom.

Appendix II: Consolidated List of Aircraft, Personnel, & Major Equipment of Forces "A," "B," & "C"

Force "A" (Parachute)

Unit	**Aircraft**	**Personnel**	**Guns**
Div Hq, 82nd ABN	9	105	
508th PIR	117	1994	
507th PIR	117	2004	
505th PIR	117	2095	2 75mm Pack How
307th Abn Engr	9	144	
82nd Abn P/F Grps	9	54	
TOTAL	**378**	**6396**	

Force "B" (Glider)

Unit	**A/C**	**Personnel**	**Guns**	**Trks 1/4T**	**TLRS**	**M/C**
Div Hq, 82nd Abn	19	185		12	9	4
82nd Abn Rcn Plat	13	49		9		4
82nd Abn Div Arty	11	50		4	3	
82nd Abn Sign Co	13	82		7	4	5
80th Abn AA Bn	57	226	24 57 mm	27	15	
307th Abn Med Co	20	144		18	14	
307th Abn Engr Bn	10	99		5	3	
319th GFA bn	40	362	12 75mm	32	17	
320th GFA Bn	54	343	12†105mm How	30	20	
325th GIR	129	1841	9 57 mm AT	28	15	
2nd Bn, 401 GI	43	459		6	5	
Comd vehs, 505, 507, 508 PIRs	15	24		13		
ASP	4	5		2		
TOTAL	428	3871		193	105	13

Force "C" (Seaborne)

Unit	**Pers**	**2 1/2 t Trk**	**1t Tlr**	**1 1/2 Trk**	**3/4 t W/C**	**2 1/2 t Dump**	**75mm How**	**3/4 t Amb**	**1/4 t Trk**	**1/4 t Trl**
82d Abn Hq	70	1	6	7	1					
505	83									
507	78									
508	64									
325	77			9						
82 Arty	19	3	3		1					
319	47	3	3		13					
320	50	3	3	12	1					
456	471	15	15		18		10		27	18
80 AA	258			24					12	6
307	65	2	2			4				
Sig Corp	17	1	1	1						
Med Co	26			5						
Ord Main	68	6	3						3	3
QM Co	59			1					3	3
MP Pl	30			1					3	3
3809 QM	115	53							3	
3810 QM	115	53							3	
Totals:	1712	140	37	60	34	4	10	8	56	33

Force "B" :	3871
Force "A":	6396
Total:	11,979

Appendix III: Consolidated Casualties Report Normandy Campaign

Unit	MIA	WIA	RTD	Injured	RTD	KIA	POW	Total
Hq	3	7	7	4	2	1		
Hq Co	1	10	8	4	4	12		
MP Pl		1	1					
504								
505	60	492	353	164	129	186	51	
507	337	526	270	96	56	251	4	
508	192	487	313	118	83	315	93	
325	24	483	351	162	108	200	12	
82 Art		3	2			1		
319	1	40	2	41	32	27		
320		29	21	27	17	22		
376								
456		14	10	5	4	8		
80 AA	8	28	22	22	18	14	3	
307	19	30	18	3	3	17	15	
407								
Sig C	9	4	2	17	12	11	1	
Med C	1	3	2	3	2	4		
782		1	1	1	1			
401	6	210	149	37	32	74		
Total:	661	2373	1554	704	502	1142	179	3003

Appendix IV: Air Movement Tables

1. Air Mouvement table – Parachute

Serial	**Airborne Unit**	**No A/C**	**Takeoff** Airfield	DZ	DZ time
4	82nd Pathfinders	3	N.Witham	O	0121
5	82nd Pathfinders	3	N.Witham	N	0138
6	82nd Pathfinders	3	N.Witham	T	0202
	Mission *Boston* (D-Day)				
17	2 Bn 505th PIR	36	Cottesmore	O	0151
18	3 Bn 505th PIR	36	Cottesmore	O	0157
	2 Secs. 456th PFA				
19	1st Bn 505th PIR	36	Spanhoe	O	0203
	Hq&Hq Co 505	9			
	Plat 307 Abn Engr	9			
	Det. Hq 82 Abn Div				
20	2 Bn 508th PIR	36	Saltby	N	0208
21	Hq& Hq Co 508th	9			
	Co B 307th Engr	6			
	Force "A" Hq	9	Saltby	N	0214
22	1 Bn 508th PIR	36	Folkingham	N	0220
23	3 Bn 508th PIR	36	Folkingham	N	0226
24	2 Bn 507th PIR	36	Barkston	T	0232
25	3 Bn 507th PIR	36	Barkston	T	0238
26	1 Bn 507th PIR	36			
	Hq&Hq Co 507th	9	Fulbock	T	0244
	Mission *Freeport* (D plus one, Resupply)				
26	Resupply	47	Barkston Heath	O	0611
39	Resupply	46	Folkingham	0	0617
40	Resupply	46	Saltby	O	0623
41	Resupply	46	Cottesmore	O	0629

2. Air Movement table – Glider

Serial	Airborne unit	No A/C	Gliders: CG4A	Horsa	LZ	Takeoff Airfield	LZ Time
	Mission *Detroit* (D-Day)						
28	Btrys A&B B 80 Abn AA Bn	52	42		O	Ramsbury	0400
	Hq 82 Abn Div		6				
	ASP (Glider)		1				
	82 Abn Div Arty		1				
	82 Abn Sig Co		2				
	Mission *Elmira* (D-Day)						
30	Btry C 80 Abn AA Bn	26		13	W	Ramsbury	2110
	Hq 82 Abn Div			4			
	Cmd Veh, Div Hq		3				
	82 Abn Sig Corp		1				
	ASP (Glider)		1				
	82 Abn Div Arty		1	1			
	Hq 80 Abn AA Bn		2				
31	307 Abn Med Corps	50		18	W	Greeham Commons	2120
	82 Rcn Plat		11				
	82 Abn Sig Corps		1	9			
	Hq 82 Abn Div			9			
	ASP vehicles		2				
32	319 GFA Bn	50		40	W	Membury	2300
	320 GFA Bn			4			
	82 Abn Div Arty		1	2			
	307 Abn Med Corps		1	1			
	Co A 307 Abn			1			
33	320 GFA Bn	50	12	38	W	Welford	2310
	Mission *Gaveston* (D plus one)						
34	1 Bn 325 GIR	50	28	15	W	Ramsbury	0700
	Co A 307 Abn Engr		4	3			
35	Hq& Hq Co 325 GIR	50	40		W	Aldermaston	0710
	82 Abn Div Arty		5				
	Co A 307 Abn Engr		2				
	82 Abn Recon Plat		2				
	Cnd Veh 508 PIR		1				
	Mission *Hackensack* (D plus one)						
36	2 Bn 325th GIR	50	10	15	W	Uppotery	0900
	2 Bn 401th GIR		10	15			
37	2 Bn 325th GIR Sply	50	18				0910
	2 Bn 401th GIR		18				
	Serv.Co 325th GIR		3				
	Cmd Veh 505,507,508		11				

The Supercommandos
First Special Service Force, 1942-1944
An Illustrated History
Robert Todd Ross

Chronicles the organization, training, and combat operations of the First Special Service Force during its brief but exhilarating history. Full-color maps, Order of Battle graphics, charts, and numerous noteworthy original Force documents are also included. Over eighty full-color images of authentic First Special Service Force uniforms, insignia, weapons and equipment. An invaluable resource for any collector, reenactor, veteran, or historian.
Size: 8 1/2" x 11" ■ over 600 b/w photographs, over eighty color photographs, maps, documents ■ 320 pp
ISBN: 0-7643-1171-9 ■ hard cover ■ $59.95

With The Black Devils
A Soldier's World War II Account
with the First Special Service Force
and the 82nd Airborne
Mark J. Nelson

With The Black Devils offers readers a rare first-hand account of life with an elite group of American and Canadian World War II soldiers known as the First Special Service Force or "Black Devils". Based on the letters and diary entries of Sam Byrne, who served with the Force from the early days in Montana through the unit's inactivation in France, the book shares the thoughts and emotions of a front line soldier chronicling his activities as they take place. The book follows Sam's experiences after the Force's breakup, as he served in both the 504th and 507th Parachute Infantry Regiments. The author surrounds Sam's letters and diary entries with background information thereby placing Sam's words into a meaningful context for the reader. This book will appeal to anyone with an interest in World War II in general or the First Special Service Force specifically.
Size: 6"x9" ■ 30 b/w photographs ■ 176 pp
ISBN: 0-7643-2054-8 ■ hard cover ■ $29.95